TEACHING AS A PROFESSION

To David, Juliet and Sally

GLENN LANGFORD

Teaching as a profession

An essay in the philosophy of education

**Manchester
University Press**

© GLENN LANGFORD 1978

Published by Manchester University Press
Oxford Road, Manchester M13 9PL

ISBN 0 7190 0717 8

British Library cataloguing in publication data
Langford, Glenn
  Teaching as a profession.
  1. Teaching – Philosophy
  I. Title
  371.1'02'01   LB1025.2

ISBN 0–7190–0717–8

Computerised Phototypesetting by
G C Typeset Ltd., Bolton, Greater Manchester
Printed in Great Britain by A. Wheaton & Co., Ltd., Exeter

CONTENTS

ACKNOWLEDGEMENTS

I have benefited greatly, in thinking about the subject matter of this book, from discussions with colleagues, friends and students. I am also most grateful to Mrs Peggy Martin for her patience and efficiency in connection with the preparation of the typescript.

CHAPTER ONE

Education and teaching

1
INTRODUCTION

This book is about education and teaching and the way they are related when teaching is thought of as a profession. My remarks are for the most part general in nature and to some extent apply also to other professions. Examples other than teaching are referred to, therefore, both for their intrinsic interest and for the light that they throw on the idea of teaching as a profession.

My approach is philosophical in the sense that it is concerned with ideas rather than with the facts of particular situations. I have taken the view that education and teaching cannot be understood unless they are thought of as social phenomena; and that social phenomena, in turn, cannot be understood unless they are related to their social context. For reasons which are explained in the next section, I begin in chapter two with an account of a profession. This is followed, in chapter three, with an account of the nature of social phenomena and, in chapters four and five, with an attempt to understand how different kinds of social phenomena – individual persons, social groups and communities – differ from and are related to one another. There is also, in chapter five, an attempt to say how a profession is related to the community of which it is a part. The profession which I have in mind throughout is teaching; and chapter four includes sections on 'What is education?' and on educational theory.

This book has been written against the background of contemporary writing in the philosophy of education and is to some extent a reaction against it. In writing it I have not felt obliged to adhere to any one philosophical method. I do not consider the traditional empiricist metaphysic of atomism adequate for an understanding of the nature of social phenomena nor, therefore, the method of analysis associated with it particularly suitable. The method I have adopted would therefore be better described as descriptive or phenomonological rather than analytic.

2
EDUCATION AND TEACHING

I want to begin by considering, briefly, the connection between teaching and education and the kind of account which is given of each in contemporary writing in the philosophy of education in the predominant empiricist, atomistic tradition in Anglo-American philosophy. The question 'What is teaching?' is interpreted primarily as a question about isolated transactions between individuals considered only as parties to those transactions rather than as a question about the activity of teachers considered as a social group. Consequently the questions 'What is teaching?' and 'What is education?' are treated as separate questions or as related only contingently. There may as a matter of fact be a connection between teaching and education; but it is not necessary to refer to education in order to define teaching. To teach is to help (or, strictly, to try to help) someone to learn something; and what is learnt need make no contribution to the learner's education. For example, people teach their dogs to walk to heel, their friends to play pontoon and their children to make daisy chains, without thereby necessarily contributing in any way to their education. They may do so or they may not; but whether they do depends on further considerations beyond those which lead us to say that they are teaching.

Even if this conclusion is accepted, however, it need not follow that there is nothing further to be said about the connection between teaching and education. According to the definition of teaching given above, the teacher need not intend what is learnt to make a contribution to the learner's education; but there is no reason why he should not in fact intend it to do so. Moreover, if the teacher is a professional teacher in the sense of being someone who earns his living as a teacher in a school, college or university, there is every reason why he should so intend, since schools, colleges and universities are educational institutions. If therefore teaching is thought of in terms of the activities of a social group rather than in terms of isolated transactions there is after all a strong connection between teaching and education. Teaching is what teachers do; and teachers work in institutions the purpose of which is concerned with education. Indeed, their work might be said to be constitutive of such institutions.

It cannot be denied, however, that some teaching has very little connection with education, even when undertaken by full-time teachers; for example, teaching in language schools in which English is taught as a foreign language. My own view, which I will try to develop in the following pages, is that the relevant connection is not between teaching as such and education but between teaching as a profession and education. That is, that the learning which teachers who are members of the teaching profession try to bring about is that which leads to education. I conclude that it is teaching as a profession and not teaching as such which is of most direct concern to the philosopher of education. The central questions for philosophy of education, therefore, are first, what is a profession and, secondly, what is distinctive of teaching as a profession. As I have already indicated, the brief answer to the second question is its concern for education. If this approach is adopted, the question 'What is education?' is arrived at only in the course of considering the nature of the activities of professional teachers and cannot profitably be raised in abstraction from the context of such activities.

I propose to begin, in the next chapter, therefore, with an account of what a profession is.

CHAPTER ONE: NOTES AND REFERENCES
(numbers correspond to numbers of sections)

2. In *The Logic of Education*, for example, Professors P. H. Hirst and R. S. Peters say that 'learning is logically necessary to education, whereas teaching is not' (p. 77). On their view, therefore, it makes sense to begin by saying what education is and then go on to ask whether what goes on in

educational institutions is in fact education. Similarly, according to the definition of teaching given by Professor Israel Scheffler in *The Language of Education* and followed by Peters in *Ethics and Education*, it makes sense to ask whether what teachers, including professional teachers, do is in fact teaching. According to my own view (put forward in *Philosophy and Education* and elaborated in 'The concept of education' in *New Studies in the Philosophy of Education*) education is best understood as a practical social activity the overall purpose of which is to help others to learn to become persons.

I gave an account of teachers and teaching in chapters 8 and 9 of *Philosophy and Education*. There is a perceptive discussion of teaching by Professor Hirst in 'What is teaching?', reprinted from *Journal of Curriculum Studies*, vol. 3, 1971, in *The Philosophy of Education*, edited by R. S. Peters. In it he refers incidentally to teachers as forming a profession; but he is primarily concerned with distinguishing teaching from other closely related acts by reference to their internal nature. My own view is that acts are identified as teaching acts by reference to their overall purpose or, to put it another way, by reference to their context within a more complex purposive activity.

CHAPTER TWO

The nature of a profession

My remarks about the nature of a profession fall under the headings of (1) payment, (2) knowledge and skills, (3) responsibility and purpose, (4) the professional ideal of service, (5) unity and (6) recognition. The considerations falling under each heading are not independent of one another; and one of the things which I will try to do is to bring out the relations between them.

1
PAYMENT

A professional, as contrasted with an amateur, usually gets paid for what he does; and, in some cases at least, we mean no more than this when we say of someone that he is a professional. We use the word 'professional' in this restricted way, however, only when there is some point in doing so. For example, a professional decorator is one who earns his living by painting and decorating, in contrast with an impoverished owner-occupier who paints his house out of necessity. Similarly, athletes are classified as professionals because they accept, or even have at some time accepted, payment; whereas most people who play games and take part in athletics do not receive payment. On the other hand, we have no reason to speak of professional train drivers because almost all train drivers get paid. But we would describe those who don't get paid – for example, railway enthusiasts who keep open, on a non-commercial basis, a branch line which would otherwise be closed – as amateurs.

The use of the word 'professional' simply to describe someone who provides a service for payment is not in itself of much interest. Even if it is sometimes used in this restricted way, it is not often that this is all that is meant. Amateur athletes, for example, compete only against other amateurs, and professionals only against other professionals; and the use of the word 'professional', when applied to athletes, would be taken to include a reference to this fact. More generally, there is every reason to expect a professional to be better at what he does than an amateur, since he usually spends more time at it than someone who has to earn his living elsewhere. Also, one reason why we are prepared to pay people to do things is that they are good at them; the payment criterion, therefore, is often used in conjunction with the next criterion to be considered, that of skill. In some cases, however, the question of whether the performance of the professional is necessarily superior to that of the amateur is left open. People may service their own cars, for example, because they do not feel they can trust the garage to do a proper job.

The fact that professionals, including teachers, do normally get paid for what they do, however, is important, even although we usually mean to convey much more by the use of the word 'professional'. The receipt of payment is one side of a contract or bargain, the other side of which is the performance of the services contracted for. A professional teacher is not simply one who does as a matter of fact teach but also one who has a duty to teach. Since the duty arises out of a contract it is primarily a legal duty, although most people would agree with Locke that 'the keeping of faith' is also morally required of us. What the teacher is required to do in the performance of his duty is laid down by the terms of his contract; it will obviously include teaching but may include other things as well. And his duty is owed to the other party to the contract, that is, to his employer.

At this point, the economists' distinction between the public and the private sectors of the economy is relevant. Most teachers are employed by local or central government, and, therefore, belong to the public sector, although a minority are employed by private institutions, for example, the so-called public schools, or even by private individuals. Two things follow from this; first, that most teachers are employed, directly or indirectly, by the community. Secondly, the public sector typically, although not exclusively, produces services rather than tangible products which can be bought and sold in the market place; and these services are rendered not only to particular individuals but also to the community at large. It is the recognition of this fact which accounts for the enormous expansion in the public sectors of almost all advanced countries today. It is part of the job of the health service, for example, to combat epidemics, not simply to treat individuals; and similarly, it is part of the job of the teaching profession to minimise illiteracy, not simply to teach individuals to read.

I said above that a professional teacher's duty is owed to his employer. It might be objected that whereas this is so in the case of other employees, a teacher's duty is to the children he teaches. But, though professional teachers do have a special concern for the children they teach, which will be considered later, it is a mistake to think of that concern as a duty which arises out of a contract of employment. For the same reason a doctor's concern for his patients cannot be wholly explained by pointing to the fees which he is paid. The objection is less plausible if the content of a duty is distinguished from the person to whom the duty is owed. A teacher employed to teach the children of a particular school has a duty to teach them, just as the painter employed to paint the school building has a duty to paint it. But it no more follows that the teacher has a duty to the children than the painter has to the school building, except in a derivative sense; his duty, in the contractual sense, is to his employer. He *may* have a duty to them; but if so it is not a legal duty but a duty of a different kind.

2
KNOWLEDGE AND SKILLS

In considering payment I pointed out that there is every reason to expect a professional to become proficient at what he does in order to earn his living. Even in the simplest tasks performance improves with practice; and very few tasks are so simple that there are no skills to be acquired or tricks to be learnt. But there are big differences in the extent to which knowledge and skills are required for efficient performance; and these are reflected in the classification of workers into unskilled, semi-skilled and skilled. Possession of skills which are both socially useful and difficult to acquire tends to set those who possess them apart, giving them higher status and better pay than other workers. Because of what in fact they have in common they may come to think of themselves as a group; and if so are likely to co-operate with one another through formal trade associations. The primary purpose of such associations will be to protect and promote the common interests of their members, both as they relate to the efficient practice of their trade and to their desire to receive adequate payment for their services. They may, for example, regulate conditions of entry to and numbers entering the trade, most obviously by requiring those who wish to enter to undergo a period of apprenticeship or to pass examinations. They may also represent their members in negotiations with employers about rates of pay and other conditions of employment.

The knowledge and skill required for the efficient practice of a profession, however, differ from those required for the practice of a trade not only in extent but also in kind. In general, the tradesman or technician knows how to do what needs to be done and, very often, what needs to be done; but may not know why it should be done. He acts according to a rule of thumb, doing things the way he learnt as an apprentice, the way they have always been done. Tradition is his only guide; and, since it is the end-product of a process of trial and error extending over many generations, it is in general a satisfactory guide. On the other hand, in some cases it may be possible not only to know how a desired result may be achieved but also why it can be achieved in that way. All trades and professions depend in practice on a mixture of tradition and understanding; but in so far as there is scope for understanding in a particular area of activity it is the members of the relevant profession rather than trade who would be expected to have it.

The knowledge and skill required for a profession, therefore, include whatever theoretical knowledge is available. Such knowledge can be acquired only through study and training over a period of years; and professional training cannot even begin until a certain minimum standard of general education has been attained. Anyone wanting to enter a profession has to continue his full-time education for several years after the normal school leaving age and then embark upon an arduous course of professional training. A professional qualification, therefore, represents a considerable financial and intellectual investment both for the individual concerned and the community. For this reason, if for no other, entering a profession is a long-term commitment; it is a choice of livelihood, a settled preference for making a living in a particular way. A further sense in which a choice of profession involves a commitment will be brought out later.

Before moving on, I will try to say a little about the knowledge and skill requirement as applied to teaching. In the introduction I suggested that there is a connection between teaching as a profession (though not teaching as such) and education. If this is correct – a question which will be considered later – professional teaching qualifications fall under three headings: pedagogy, content and education. So far as pedagogy is concerned, the distinction between knowing how to achieve a desired result – in this case, learning – and knowing why it can be achieved in that way is obviously important. The routine application of rules of thumb can be relied upon to produce the desired result only within a restricted range of circumstances. But the circumstances in which the professional teacher finds himself vary: from class to class within the same school, from one school to another and even, within a highly fluid educational system such as our own, from one generation of students to another. The teacher has to deal with people; and people differ from one another far more than, for example, people's bodies, farm animals or building sites. Understanding of teaching principles therefore is highly desirable in so far as there are principles available to be understood. Unfortunately it is not obvious that there are any principles of teaching to be understood; nor, if there are, what account is to be given of them. So far as content is concerned, the teacher will himself need to know at least most of what he is trying to help others to learn; the science teacher will need to know some science, the maths teacher some maths and so on. Finally, in so far as the professional teacher is concerned with the education of others, he ought above all to be educated himself. This point cannot be emphasised too much, in view of the modern obsession with technique. A man who is himself uneducated is unlikely to contribute to anyone else's education. If he does so it will be unintentionally, either by chance or under the guidance of someone else who is educated. This is simply because he will have no clear idea of what the object of the exercise is supposed to be; and gadgetry for its own sake is a waste of time and money. There is, then, no sharp contrast between professional teacher training and education, although there may be in the case of other professions. Being educated is a professional qualification for teaching in a way in which it isn't for other professions; indeed, it is *the* professional qualification for teaching. On the other hand there is no reason why teacher training in the narrow sense of instruction in pedagogy and the acquisition of content should not contribute to the teacher's education. My remarks in this paragraph would normally be regarded as falling under the heading of educational theory. The nature of educational theory is considered later in chapter four, section 5. A further aspect of professional training is also considered in section 5 of the present chapter.

Professionals, then, usually get paid for what they do; and professional practice rests on skills and requires knowledge acquired through special training which non-members do not possess. But a conception of a profession based only on these two factors is too narrow. It fails to take account of the fact that at least a proportion of those who enter professions like medicine and teaching do so not so much because they want an interesting, well paid job but because they want to do something worth doing. Teachers think children are important as people, not just as future breadwinners; doctors care about people's health. The word 'professional' is sometimes intended to be understood in the narrower sense. A prostitute, for example, is a professional in the sense that she makes love for payment rather than for love; and a mercenary fights for personal gain, not for his country. But in other cases it is obvious that much more is intended to be understood by the use of the words 'professional' and 'profession'. The most interesting of the part of the extra which is involved, from the philosophical point of view, will be considered in the next section under the heading of responsibility.

3
RESPONSIBILITY AND PURPOSE

In order to be clear about the connection between the idea of a profession and that of responsibility the complexity and ambiguity of the notion of responsibility must be considered. There are, indeed, not one but a number of closely related concepts of responsibility which will be considered in turn.

i
RESPONSIBILITY AS AGENT

The basic notion, which is of central philosophical importance, is that of being responsible for the occurrence of an event in the sense of bringing it about or causing it to happen. All cases of bringing about may be categorised under one or the other of two headings: that of causation and that of agency. In the former case, one natural event is responsible for the occurrence of another in the sense of causing it to happen; in the latter, a person is responsible for the occurrence of an event in the sense of performing the relevant action. Although causing and acting share the notion of bringing about, and although ordinary language is frequently ambiguous as between them, the two cases are very different and it is, of course, the latter which is relevant here.

Persons, although not inanimate objects or, probably, other animals, have the ability to make or cause things to happen. From this point of view, they may be referred to as agents and, correspondingly, this sort of responsibility as agency. In acting, persons are aware of the situation in which and on which they act and of the change which they are endeavouring to bring about. They hold beliefs about the situation in which they find themselves and act in the light of those beliefs; they also have some conception of themselves as agents and of the end towards which their behaviour is directed and, therefore, of the change which they wish to initiate. Further, part of what we mean in speaking of persons as agents is that their behaviour is under their control, in the sense that they possess not only the ability to behave as they do but also the ability to refrain from behaving in that way. Their behaviour, therefore, is said to be the product of choice, they do what they do because they want to.

The basic sense, then, in which persons may be said to be responsible is that in which they may be said to bring events about intentionally; that is, in acting on, rather than in simply reacting to, the situation in which they find themselves.

ii

SOCIAL RESPONSIBILITY

It is only because, or in so far as, persons are thought to be responsible in this most basic way that it makes sense to attribute responsibility to them in a further, social sense. Human societies, institutions and activities are structured by social rules which guide and control the behaviour of their members by making it clear how they are expected and, indeed, required to behave in differing circumstances. They do not *have* to behave in the relevant way, in the sense of being caused to do so by those circumstances, since they possess the ability to refrain from behaving in that way. In so far as they fail to do so, however, they may be required to give an account of their failure and may be punished if they cannot satisfactorily do so. In short, persons, because they are responsible for what they do in the primary, agency sense, may also be held socially responsible, or accountable, for their failure to do or refrain from doing what is socially required of them.

Many social rules apply to all of the members of a society, for example the criminal law. Others are more restricted in their scope and are intended only to structure the behaviour of those occupying certain roles or engaged in certain occupations. Professional ethics are considered further in chapter four, section 3(ii) and chapter five, section 3(iv).

iii

RESPONSIBLE PERSONS

The related notions of agency and social responsibility are of very general philosophical interest and basic to any understanding of any social activity, including that of professions. There is a further notion, that of a responsible person, which has more particular relevance. A responsible person is one who does what he should simply because he sees that he should. There is no need, therefore, either for someone else to see that he does what he should or for any other form of external pressure such as a system of sanctions. If the workers on, for example, a car assembly line are not responsible in this sense it will be necessary to have an elaborate inspection system to make sure that finished cars are up to standard, to relate pay to the proportion of cars which pass inspection and so on. On the other hand the workers may accept personal responsibility for their work, making such arrangements unnecessary. The latter attitude seems more likely where there is scope for the worker to take pride in his work because, for example, he is able to see the finished product and to see in it a reflection of his own skill. It is preferable, therefore, from the point of view both of efficiency and of the worker's own self-respect, that the individual should accept personal responsibility for his own work. For many sorts of job, however, there is an alternative available in the form of close supervision. But this is not possible in every case; most obviously because, at some stage, responsibility must be accepted by someone for seeing that things go right; and secondly, because the amount of specialised skill and knowledge and the varied nature of the tasks involved make any form of close supervision impracticable. It is not surprising, therefore, that the worker who possesses specialised knowledge and skills and the worker who accepts personal responsibility for his own work tend to combine, in varying proportions, in the same person. Nor is it surprising that those who are both knowledgeable and responsible should also become indirectly responsible for the work of others; that is, should come to occupy supervisory and management positions. A distinction can be made between administration and management on the one hand and professional work on the other. The administrator is responsible, and accepts responsibility, for long-term planning and co-ordination, without which the efforts of others would be wasted; whilst the manager is responsible for making sure that things go well from day to day. The professional as such is less concerned with planning and supervision and more with matters of relative detail which need his special knowledge and skill; in other words, he is a shop-floor worker rather than part of management. But administrators and managers and professionals are alike in that they share a responsible attitude to what they are doing. Moreover, the administrator will need some technical knowledge, even if only enough to understand and assess professional advice; whilst the professional often acts also as a supervisor. Hospital doctors in their relation to nurses provide a good example: doctors direct the work of nurses not because nurses are not responsible people but because doctors are better qualified to decide what needs to be done. The relationship between teachers and teaching auxiliaries is presumably intended to follow a similar pattern. How the complex of roles which I have been trying to sketch works out in detail will depend on particular cases; but it will obviously be different in, say, medicine, teaching and building.

iv

RESPONSIBILITY FOR PURPOSE

Finally there is a further connection between the notion of a profession and responsibility. Normally one person employs another because they want something doing but, for one reason or another, cannot or do not wish to do it themselves; they therefore employ someone else to do it for them. The employee may then be said to be no more than the agent of his employer, on whose behalf he acts; no purpose of his own is reflected in what he does. He is paid to become, for the period of his employment, no more than an extension of the agency of his employer. This is recognised in the law relating to master and servant, according to which, within defined limits, the actions of a servant are deemed to be the actions of his master, who is therefore responsible for them in the social or accountability sense. An employee who is no more than what I will call an agent-for-another may nevertheless act as a responsible person. Provided he is clear what his employer wants him to do, there is no reason why he should not do it to the best of his ability

whether he is being supervised or not. But in so far as he is
acting in accordance with purposes which he does not share it
would not be surprising if he did only what he was obliged to do
in order to qualify for his pay.

The distinction between employer and employee is not,
however, the same as that between agent-for-another and
principal. Whether or not he is an employee, a member of a
profession acts, to a greater or lesser degree, as a principal
acting in his own right rather than merely as an agent-for-
another. Both a principal and an agent-for-another are agents in
the basic sense that they are aware of the situation in which they
act and of the change which they intend to bring about in or
through their action. An agent-for-another, if he is a responsible
person, accepts responsibility for achieving the ends or purposes
towards which his actions are directed; but the only purpose of
his own which is involved in what he does is his desire to make a
living. A principal, on the other hand, is responsible not merely
for achieving but also for setting the ends of his actions; it is his
purposes which are reflected in what he does and not merely
those of others. It need not follow, of course, that his purposes
are not shared by other members of the same profession or of
the community to which that profession belongs.

4
THE PROFESSIONAL IDEAL OF SERVICE

I concluded, in the previous section, that a professional person,
whether an employee or not, acts as a principal in his own right
rather than as an agent-for-another. The purposes which he
strives to achieve are his own rather than laid down for him by
someone else.

It need not follow, however, that he acts in his own interests
rather than in the interests of others. On the contrary, it is an
important part of the idea of a profession that its members,
although acting as principals, nevertheless act, in their
professional capacities, in the interests of others. Doctors, for
example, want their patients to get well; lawyers want justice for
their clients; and teachers want their pupils to become educated.
Of course, they also want other things which do relate to their

own personal interest: to earn a good living, to get intellectual and emotional satisfaction from their work, to enjoy the respect of their colleagues and so on. But these are aims which are shared with those who are not members of a profession; they are not professional purposes as such.

Peculiarly professional purposes are characterised in two related ways. First, they concern the interests of others and, secondly, their concern is with a special aspect of the interest of others such as their health or education. From this point of view, the other people concerned are those who need the specialised help which the professional, because of his knowledge and skills, is able to provide. They may be thought of, collectively, as the rest of the community or, distributively, as those individuals who, from time to time, stand in need of the relevant professional help. To hold professional purposes as such, then, is to want to provide that help simply because, in your professional and therefore expert opinion, it is needed.

It is this ideal of service which lies behind the suggestion, which I considered and rejected earlier, that the teacher has a duty to the children he teaches rather than to his employer. His duty to his employer, however, is a contractual, legal duty; it is based on an agreement between the two for their mutual advantage. His concern for the children he teaches is not like that. He wants them to become educated not because, if they do, some further advantage, financial or emotional, will come to him but simply because that is what he wants.

It is sometimes denied that disinterestedness, in the sense indicated above, is possible. The questions which arise, if this suggestion is taken seriously, are complex and I will return to them in the first section of the next chapter. I do not, however, wish to deny that professional people, including teachers, have private as well as professional lives to live. A member of a profession, therefore, may find himself in a situation of conflict when the dictates of self-interest or, indeed, duty to his employer, fail to coincide with strictly professional purposes. A dentist, for example, may have to decide whether to fill or extract a tooth. His professional regard for dental health may suggest a filling or a crown, even though an extraction would be more profitable to him or less costly to the health service. A conflict of this sort provides a test of professional integrity; there is no reason to suppose that professional people are completely lacking in self-interest. In teaching, too, there is a conflict between getting on – referred to, with unconscious irony, as profesional advancement – and getting on with the job; in other words, between personal and professional considerations. In a university this may take the form of writing papers in order to secure tenure or promotion rather than in order to say something worth saying. The latter activitity may be complementary to university teaching; the former serves no good purpose beyond the limited one of desire for personal security or advancement. In practice motives are almost always mixed; and things may be arranged so that the conduct dictated by personal and by professional purposes coincides. Nevertheless the distinction between the two kinds of purpose remains.

5
UNITY

A member of a profession, then, accepts responsibility not merely for achieving certain purposes but also for setting up those purposes. Nothing I have said so far, however, explains why we think of the members of a profession as forming a unity in being united in one profession. The members of a profession not only, individually, adopt professional purposes; they also adopt the same purposes and, moreover, realise that they share the same purposes and co-operate with one another in order to achieve them. The unity of a profession depends primarily on the sense of purpose which its members share and are aware of sharing. Nor is it difficult to explain how this comes about. A recruit may be attracted to a profession because he feels he would like to help achieve the purposes which he knows the profession has; or in the course of his professional training he comes to adopt those purposes. He acquires not just the knowledge and skills which he needs in order to practise his chosen profession but also to think and feel like a member of that profession.

This side of professional training is of the utmost importance.

It has two aspects. First, the newcomer has to find out what those purposes are; and, secondly, he has to make them his own. They have to become *his* purposes, not simply purposes which other members of the profession have and which he knows he is supposed to share. These two requirements are not independent of each other. The first is clearly a necessary although not a sufficient condition of the latter. It can, to some extent, be achieved by instruction; indeed, it is, or ought to be, a principal function of philosophy of education to help to do this for the teaching profession. The second can hardly be achieved by according it a special place in the college curriculum, although this may have been the idea behind the more traditional sort of philosophy of education. Rather the ethos of a profession is implicit in everything that is said and done in, for example, a college of education or a teaching hospital.

Since professional purposes are acquired and reinforced in this social way, the members of a profession not only share the same purposes but are also aware of the fact that they share them. Members of a profession are therefore likely to form associations through which their shared view of the purpose of their profession can find articulation. In being articulated, that view is likely to be clarified, refined and strengthened. Professional associations may also contribute to the achievement of the purposes of the profession by providing facilities for members, such as technical information services, sponsoring and financing research, representing the profession in discussions with government, in public debate and in the public press.

The claim that professional teachers share a common purpose appears to be refuted by the obvious fact of disagreement within the teaching profession on fundamental matters; but I do not think that this is so. First, in order to refer to the teaching profession, if only to say that its members often disagree, what we are talking about must be identified in some way; and the only principle of identity available, so far as I can see, is provided by the purpose which the members of the profession share. Secondly, meaningful disagreement is possible only between those whose outlooks do not differ too radically; there must be some common ground if disagreement is to be possible.

Thirdly, it may be part of the purpose of the teaching profession to foster critical attitudes in others; it would not be wholly surprising, therefore, in teachers, if only to a limited extent, practised what they preached. Fourthly, an open-minded, critical attitude may serve to improve social institutions; this is the assumption behind Benthamite utilitarianism. But if it gets out of hand it can also destroy them; the price of critical rationalism in social matters is an increase in the instability of social institutions. The teaching profession is in fact a changing profession; and it could be the case, although I do not think that it is, that it is in the process of disintegrating. In this respect medicine is more favourably placed; it is not simply that it is easier to say what the purpose of medicine is but that radical disagreement about the desirability of saving life is ruled out by the almost universal desire to stay alive.

6
RECOGNITION

The members of a profession not only see themselves as members of a profession but are also seen as a profession by the rest of the community; and recognition as a profession is desired by its members. They think that they have something of value to offer to the community; and in recognising them as a profession the community is agreeing that this is so. Recognition, therefore, carries with it social status. Recognising the value of the service provided, the community is also more willing to pay for it. This does not follow directly. Doctors, for example, are paid well whereas nurses, whose work is closely connected, are not. But it does usually. Professional people, therefore, tend to be well paid; the idea of a profession carries with it a middle-class glow of comfort, safety and prosperity.

Finally, in being recognised as both skilled and responsible, the members of a profession are more likely to be allowed to get on with the job as they see it without interference. They are the people who know best what needs to be done and how to do it; and, from the standpoint of the community, they are the people most concerned to see that it is done and done well. We are, of course, all concerned about our own health and education and that of our children; it is primarily the doctor and the teacher who are concerned about the health and education of the community and its children.

Recognition as a profession, then, brings with it increased social prestige, better pay and independence.

7
CONCLUSION

I have tried to give some account of the nature of a profession according to which a profession is identified primarily by reference to the purpose which its members share and by the specialised knowledge and skill necessary for its achievement. Doctors, for example, want their patients to get well and have the knowledge and skill necessary to help them to do so; teachers want their pupils to become educated and, in the same way, can help them to do so, and so on.

In giving that account, I have tried to take into account the way that the words 'profession' and 'professional' are ordinarily used. The amount of help which can be obtained in that way, however, is limited. The point is not simply that words like 'profession' and 'professional' have tended to lose descriptive meaning, retaining only their honorific overtones. It is that they do not carry the same burden of descriptive meaning in every context in which they are used. What we mean when we describe a doctor as a professional is different from what we mean when we describe a prostitute as a professional. It is not simply that the former expresses a favourable attitude whereas the latter is pejorative. The description content of what is said itself differs. For example, when applied to the former, 'professional' means the same as 'member of a profession'; but when applied to the latter it does not. If Mrs Warren had a profession it was that of courtesan, not of prostitute. And there are other, if less obvious, differences in the use of the word 'professional' as applied to doctors, teachers, soldiers, interior decorators and so on. One cannot , therefore, expect a neat, systematic account of what the word 'professional' means which will cover all cases and which can be expressed in the form of a definition which is analytically true.

There is nevertheless a close family resemblance between the different ways in which the words 'professional' and 'profession' are used, which I have tried to keep in mind. But I have not tried to explore it in detail. I am not primarily interested in extended or marginal uses of the word 'professional', nor even in arguing about which are the marginal and which the central uses. My intention has been to describe a complex kind of social phenomenon; and not to provide individually necessary and jointly sufficient conditions for the use of the word 'profession'.

CHAPTER TWO: NOTES AND REFERENCES

Although sociologists have interested themselves in the professions, the subject has not, so far as I know, attracted the attention of contemporary philosophers. But Aristotle, in the *Nicomachean Ethics*, and F. H. Bradley in 'My station and its duties' in his *Ethical Studies* were interested in the kind of question discussed in this book. There is a brief account of a profession along similar lines to that given here in *The Role of the Teacher* by Eric Hoyle. Teacher accountability is discussed by Hugh Sockett in 'Teacher accountability' and by J. P. White in 'Teacher accountability and school autonomy' in the *Proceedings of the Philosophy of Education Society of Great Britain*, vol. X, July 1976.

2. Scepticism about the present and even future availability of scientifically based principles of teaching is expressed by Professor D. J. O'Connor in 'The nature and scope of educational theory', in *New Essays in the Philosophy of Education*, although I do not fully share his view.

3. The ideas presented in (i) and (ii) are developed more fully in chapter one of my book *Human Action*.

A distinction between work and labour, similar to that between agent-for-another and principal, is developed by P. Herbst in 'Work, labour and university education' in the Oxford *Readings in the Philosophy of Education* edited by R. S. Peters.

4. The coincidence of interest and duty was strongly recommended by Jeremy Bentham, who referred to it as the 'duty-and-interest-junction' principle. It would seem prudent to employ this principle where possible. It is not, however, always possible; nor is it true that people do not have other motives for doing their duty in those situations in which it cannot be applied.

A profession as
a social phenomenon

1
PSYCHOLOGICAL HEDONISM

In the previous chapter I drew attention to some of the distinctions which people have in mind when they use the words 'profession' and 'professional'. My remarks fell under the headings of (1) payment, (2) knowledge and skills, (3) responsibility and purpose, (4) the professional ideal of service, (5) unity and (6) recognition.

Once the work of clarification has been completed, it seems as though it is simply a question of fact whether a particular group of people form a profession. If so it could be answered, at least in principle, by conducting the appropriate enquiry. It might be objected, however, that we know *a priori* – that is, without conducting any such enquiry – that no group of people could form a profession. I said in the previous chapter that professional purposes are concerned not with the interests of those whose purposes they are but with the interests of others. It is sometimes claimed, however, that people always act for the sake of their own interests and never for the sake of the interests of others. This view is usually referred to as psychological hedonism. (In other versions, it is claimed that people always act for the sake of happiness or to maximise pleasure or minimise pain; these involve additional complications which are not relevant here.) If it were true it would follow *a priori* – in advance of examination of particular cases – that no group of people could constitute a profession as defined earlier, since the disinterested attitude required for this to be the case would be psychologically impossible. I propose, therefore, to try to show that it is not true.

Psychological hedonism is put forward as a universal truth about human nature: that is, as an empirical discovery about something which, conceivably, could have been otherwise. It is held that, as a matter of constant and universal experience, people always act for the sake of their own interest. The words 'universal' and 'always' are important. The claim is that all people, not just some or even most people, act for the sake of their own interest; and that they do so on every occasion on which they act, not just on some or even on most such occasions. It is not in any way contentious that people do normally act for the sake of their own interest, for example when they eat because they are hungry or put a coat on because they are cold; nor that there are biological grounds for taking this sort of case as standard. There is no reason why people should not act in their own interest in such cases; on the contrary, there is every reason why they should do so. In general, they are better placed than anyone else both to know where their interests lie and to further them. Nor can it be denied that people often consider only their own interest when they ought to consult the interests of others; in other words, that people often act selfishly. For example, a president or prime minister may conduct the affairs of the country primarily with a view to securing his own re-election rather than in the interests of the nation. Similarly, as was pointed out in the previous chapter, purely personal and professional considerations may conflict, and, when they do, particular individuals may give priority to the former rather than the latter.

Psychological hedonism, then, is the view that people always act for the sake of their own interest, even when there is good reason why they should consult the interests of others. To put it the other way around, it is the view that disinterested action – including, therefore, the sort of action which displays professional purpose – is psychologically impossible. Since it is a view about a question of psychological fact, it should be possible to refute it by producing evidence; and, since it is put forward as a universal truth, the evidence of a single counter-instance should suffice. All that is needed is a single example of a disinterested action; and that, it might be supposed, would be easy enough to produce. Indeed, on the face of it there are so many examples to choose from that it is arbitrary to point to one rather than another. For convenience, therefore, I will use the example of an anonymous gift to charity.

In practice the actual choice of example turns out to be unimportant. The advocate of psychological hedonism does not deny that examples of apparently disinterested actions can be found; rather he refuses to agree that they are genuinely disinterested. The person making an anonymous gift to charity, for example, does not get anything in exchange for his money, since he is making a gift, not a purchase; nor does he acquire a reputation for generosity or receive the gratitude of those he helps, since his gift is anonymous. Nevertheless, it is claimed, his action is not disinterested. He does what he does because he wants to; indeed, if he didn't want to then he wouldn't do it. On closer examination his own interests are, after all, being served by what he does, since he has the satisfaction of doing what he wants to do. The reason why the actual choice of example is unimportant, therefore, is that no evidence is allowed to count against psychological hedonism.

If no evidence is allowed to count against it, however, then no evidence can count in its favour either. It is not, as it at first appeared to be, a statement of psychological fact the truth of which depends on the evidence for or against it. Some alternative account must, therefore, be given of its logical status. One way to understand it is as a recommendation to approach the facts of human nature in a certain way; that is, without benefit of the distinction between selfish and disinterested actions. We are not, however, compelled to accept this recommendation by the weight of the evidence in its favour, since there cannot be any evidence. Moreover, the distinction between selfish and disinterested actions is one for which we have a use and which for the most part we have no difficulty in making. It is true that we are often unsure whether someone is acting selfishly or in a disinterested way. Our uncertainty arises, however, from the possibility of deception, for which there is an obvious motive, and the complexity of actual circumstances. In other cases we can and do apply the distinction with reasonable certainty. Pointing to the possibility of uncertainty, therefore, does nothing to support the contention that the distinction can never really be made. Psychological hedonism, then, is false if it is interpreted as a genuine empirical hypothesis; on the other hand, if no counter-examples are admitted it cannot be falsified but is no longer an empirical hypothesis. If it is interpreted as a recommendation about the use of words, however, then there is no reason why that recommendation should be accepted.

The attraction of psychological hedonism is partly due to an equivocation between these two positions. It is put forward as an empirical hypothesis about human nature but it is plausible only if interpreted as a recommendation about the use of words. This does not, however, explain why the temptation to equivocate in this way should be so great. The explanation is, I think, that there is a truth of a sort involved in psychological hedonism. I will try to show what this is. In the example given above, the grounds for claiming that an anonymous gift to charity was, contrary to initial appearances, not disinterested were that the person who made the gift did so because he wanted to do so. That he wanted to is not in dispute; it is an essential part of the example. And this was taken as evidence, of a sort which would also be available in the case of any other example which might be produced, that the person concerned acted in his own interests rather than in the interests of anyone else.

It is this last step which is mistaken. The mistake rests on a failure to distinguish between two apparently similar statements; first, that people always act for the sake of their own interest; and, secondly, that people always do what they want to do. The first statement is, as it is taken to be, an empirical statement about human nature which, according to the evidence, is either true or false. If the second statement is understood in the same way, however, it is not obvious that it is true; indeed, as the word 'want' is normally used it is false to say that people want to do everything which as a matter of fact they do freely. It must, therefore, be understood as a logical truth about the nature of human action and its connection with wanting; nothing is allowed to count as an action unless the person who performed it wanted to do what he did. It is then being used to draw attention to an aspect of actions which all actions necessarily share. It cannot, therefore, be used as evidence in favour of an empirical conclusion, based on experience, about the actual motives from which men act.

The truth involved in psychological hedonism, then, is that it is logically rather than psychologically impossible for a person to perform an action which he does not want to perform. For it to be true, the word 'do' must be understood in the relevant sense, that introduced in section 3(i) of the previous chapter. In this sense, people are responsible as agents for what they do. A person who does something, in the sense of causing something to happen, could have refrained from doing what he did if he had wanted to. To say 'I did it because I wanted to' claims that what happened did not just happen; it happened because I caused it to happen; and I caused it to happen because I wanted it to happen. In other words, my agency was involved; it was an action of *mine*. In so far as a person does something in their capacity as a human agent, then, it follows that they wanted to do what they did.

The word 'want', then, is used to characterise what happened as the action of a rational man, an agent who has reasons for doing one thing rather than another and who freely chose to do what he did; but it is not used to say what his reason is. Nor does the word 'free' as used here discriminate between actions any more than the word 'want'. There are no actions which are not free in the relevant sense. There are, of course, constraints on what people can do, imposed by the limits of their abilities and the circumstances, both physical and social, in which they are placed; and in practice they often have little real choice. The wage-slave, for example, is simply an agent-for-another in his work and has no real choice about whether or not to work, since the alternative is to starve. But we say that he has no real choice only because we assume that he does not want to starve; it follows, therefore, that he does want to do whatever is necessary to avoid starving. He has a choice; but we know that as a matter of fact people do not choose to starve so long as any alternative remains open to them. Similarly, the bank clerk who is ordered by a gunman to hand over the bank's money has a choice – between handing over the money and being shot – even though, as a matter of fact, we expect very few people to choose the latter alternative.

To say that a person is doing what he wants to do, therefore, is to say that he is doing it because he has a reason for what he does; it does not say what that reason is. Doctors, I said earlier, want their patients to get well; lawyers want justice for their clients; and teachers want their pupils to become educated. To say that they do what they want to do is true – indeed, logically true; and it follows that they have reasons for what they do. But it does not tell us *what* those reasons are. In so far as their reasons are characteristically professional they have already been stated as, respectively, their patients getting well, their clients receiving justice or their pupils becoming educated. They are likely, as was also admitted earlier, to have other reasons for what they do, such as earning a good salary or getting personal satisfaction from their work. What their actual reasons are is an empirical question, to be answered only be consulting the facts of particular cases. There is no single reason – whether happiness, the maximisation of pleasure or the achievement of their wants – for the sake of which men really act on every occasion on which they act at all.

The purpose of this section was to show that there is no *a priori* reason why a group of people, such as teachers, should not form a profession. I have tried, therefore, to show that psychological hedonism, which purports to offer such a reason, is mistaken.

2
THE NATURE OF SOCIAL PHENOMENA

My intention in the previous section was to show that there is no *a priori* reason why teaching should not be a profession. It does not follow, however, that whether it is is, straightforwardly, a question of fact which can be settled by observation. There are further difficulties, of a different sort, to which I would like to draw attention in this and the following sections. In doing so I hope also to throw further light on what is involved in being a profession.

The difficulties to which I would like to draw attention are a consequence of the fact that a profession is a social phenomenon. I am using the term 'social phenomena' in a very general way to refer to people and their behaviour as well as to the relations between them, the groups which they form, the activities, including professional activities, in which they participate, and the institutions which they set up; and also, although not least, to the language which they use and the observations which they make, both in their daily lives and in more disciplined contexts such as those of scientific or historical enquiry. Social phenomena characteristically possess a dimension, that of meaning, which physical phenomena lack, in consequence of which their observation is made both more difficult and more liable to error. Whether this difference is irreducible, or whether social phenomena are, in an abstract metaphysical sense, really no more than very complex physical phenomena, is irrelevant in the present context; it will certainly be reflected in any observations which anyone is ever likely to make.

We normally think of meaning as a property of words and sentences. There is no problem, therefore, about supposing that social phenomena which directly involve the use of language, for example the things which people say to one another, possess meaning. Social phenomena which do not involve the use of words, however, do involve the use of concepts; and there is a close connection between words and concepts which allows the notion of meaning to be extended to non-linguistic contexts. If anyone takes exception to this extension it need not be insisted on; the important point is that concepts are involved in social phenomena in a way in which they are not involved in physical phenomena. It is this that creates the difficulties to which I wish to draw attention.

A profession is a complex social phenomenon. Before considering it I will look at the simplest categories of social phenomena, the making of observations and behaviour. Both, perhaps, would normally be thought of as psychological rather than as social, since other people need not be involved, at least in any obvious way. I will try to show, however, that they do possess the dimension of meaning which is characteristic of social phenomena; and will then go on to consider how this affects their respective observation and, therefore, our knowledge of them.

i
OBSERVATIONS

To possess a concept, for example that of a cat or a dog, is to possess the ability to see things of the relevant sort as of that sort, that is, to see cats as cats, dogs as dogs, and so on; and, therefore, to know what it is for a thing to be a thing of that kind. An observer of any phenomenon, therefore, employs concepts in making his observations and is limited, by the concepts at his disposal, in the observations which he is able to make. For example, the observation that Chimborazo is the highest peak in the Andes can be made only by someone who possesses the concept of a mountain range, of a peak which belongs to that range, and so on. An observer would have a use for such concepts only in a world which contained mountain ranges with peaks of differing heights; indeed, he is likely to possess them only in such a world. But, irrespective of what the world contains, he will be in a position to make such an observation, in the sense of being able or having the capacity to do so in the appropriate circumstances if and when they arise, only if he possesses the relevant concepts. This point is perfectly general and applies also to observations of social phenomena. For example, the observation that a policeman is controlling the traffic at a road junction is open only to someone who knows what a policeman is, what motor cars and roads are, and so on. In these examples the concepts concerned are familiar ones which any adult possesses. But a young child or a stranger, perhaps suddenly transported from a remote part of the Amazon jungle, might not possess them; and if not would not observe what we observe, even if equally well placed, physically, to do so.

ii
OBSERVATIONS OF OBSERVATIONS

Observers, then, use concepts in making their observations. Let us now suppose that a second observer is introduced, called, for convenience, Livingstone. What Livingstone observes is the first observer, who will be called Stanley, observing that Chimborazo is the highest peak in the Andes. Stanley, as was pointed out, was able to make this observation only because he possessed certain concepts, which included that of a mountain peak. It follows that Livingstone could not make *his* observations unless he too possessed the *same* concepts, even although he is not using them in the way in which Stanley is. Stanley is observing a mountain, whereas Livingstone is observing something very different, *Stanley* observing a mountain. If, therefore, Livingstone did not possess the concept of a mountain peak and to that extent failed to share Stanley's concepts he could not have observed what he did. (He would also need to have the concept of an observer; but that is a complication which can be ignored here.) For example, if he had been hired locally to guide a cartographical expedition led by Stanley, then he might have lacked a sufficiently unified conception of the geography of South America to think in terms of continental ranges and their peaks. Nor would it be surprising if he were unaware of the purpose of the complicated measuring devices such as theodolites which Stanley would have to use. In that case, then, although in a sense he would see everything which Stanley did, he would fail to understand what he was doing. He would see the movements which Stanley made; but their meaning would be hidden from him.

Observations, then, possess a dimension of meaning in consequence of which they must be understood rather than, simply, observed.

iii

BEHAVIOUR

In the case of observations of observations it is relatively easy to see that concepts and meaning are involved in the original observations and, therefore, that the *same* concepts must be involved in *their* observation. The position is similar for observations of behaviour, provided behaviour is understood in the sense introduced in section 3 (i) of the previous chapter. Persons, it was pointed out there, possess the ability to make things happen; and what they do in exercising that ability was referred to as their actions or behaviour. Behaviour involves concepts just as much as observation, although less obviously so, and in that sense may be said to be meaningful. I will try to explain why this is so.

In order to be said to be acting, a person must be aware of the situation in which he is acting and of the way in which he intends to change that situation by his action. This is a matter of definition; nothing counts as an action unless these conditions are satisfied. The first condition, that the person be aware of the situation in which he is acting, amounts to the requirements that he hold beliefs about his situation which can then be used to guide his action. The second condition, that he be aware of the way in which he intends to change that situation, amounts to the requirement that he formulate intentions to be realised through his actions. For example, the behaviour of a man picking apples is monitored by a stream of constantly changing beliefs about the position of the apples being picked and is directed by a similar stream of intentions about the new positions which the apples are to occupy in the store cupboard. Moreover, the behaviour was what it was, and was correctly identified and described as it was — as the behaviour of a man picking apples — only because these were the beliefs and intentions which were acted on.

The beliefs and intentions which a person can have are limited by the concepts at his disposal just as much as are the observations which he can make. Indeed, beliefs are acquired and the fulfilment of intentions confirmed primarily through observation. The apple picker could not, therefore, hold the belief that there was a large rosy apple just behind his head or form the intention of picking it without bruising it unless he possessed the concepts of an apple, picking, bruising and so on. Since beliefs and intentions must be involved in anything which counts as behaviour, therefore, the behaviour open to a person is also limited by the concepts at his disposal.

iv

OBSERVATION OF BEHAVIOUR

The observation of behaviour gives rise to difficulties which are analogous to those already considered in the case of observation. Behaviour, like observation, involves the use of concepts. Two sets of concepts, therefore, are involved in the observation of behaviour: those of the person making the observation and those of the person whose behaviour is being observed. In so far, therefore, as the observer fails to share the concepts of the person whose behaviour he is observing, he cannot see it as the person sees it himself. He may see it as behaviour and, therefore, as meaningful; but he will fail to understand its actual meaning. And since the meaning is part of the phenomenon itself, he will be unable to identify it correctly.

Behaviour, then, must be understood rather than, simply, observed; and there is a corresponding possibility that it may be misunderstood. It does not follow that understanding *replaces* observation, but only that the concepts employed in making the observation must coincide with those being used in the behaviour itself. Misunderstanding also, therefore, is a kind of mis-observation which is possible only when the phenomena being observed themselves possess meaning.

It is sometimes argued, however, that behaviour cannot be observed because it involves beliefs and intentions which, in turn, cannot be observed because they are private. This view will be considered and rejected in (v) below.

v

THE PRIVACY OF BELIEFS AND INTENTIONS

It might be said that the account of behaviour given in (iii) above, which concentrated on beliefs and intentions, left out the most important part of behaviour, the bodily movements through which intentions are implemented. We would not say that the man in the apple tree was picking apples unless he reached out and grasped the apples, placed them in his backet, took them to the store room, and so on. Moreover, if beliefs and intentions are thought of as mental, in the Cartesian sense of being private to the person whose beliefs and intentions they are, they are necessarily beyond the reach of observation by a third party. Although an observer, therefore, would be able to see the man's body and the movements which he made, he would not be able to see his beliefs and intentions. He could not, therefore, observe the man's behaviour. His knowledge of the behaviour of others, if possible at all, would have to be obtained in some other way. The agent himself knows what his beliefs and intentions are without having to observe them, simply because they are his; he, therefore, is in a position to tell others what he is doing.

Alternatively, an observer might make inferences from observed bodily movement to behaviour, although with what validity might be disputed.

The claim that we can never observe the behaviour of others is in some ways like the claim that people always act in their own interests, which was considered in the previous section. In one form or another it has influenced the methodologies of sociology and psychology and worried their practitioners, just as psychological hedonism has influenced moral theory. It is important, therefore, to see why it is mistaken. If taken as an empirical hypothesis it is obviously false, since examples of such observation are readily available. It is normally obvious, for example, whether someone is picking apples. There are, it is true, occasions on which we are uncertain, puzzled or mistaken; but it does not follow that we are never in a position to observe the behaviour of others. The grounds for the claim are philosophical, therefore, and are based on a particular view of beliefs and intentions and of the way in which they are related to bodily movements in behaviour. Beliefs and intentions, on the one hand, and bodily movements, on the other, are thought of as separate entities of wholly different kinds, and consequently as related to one another in behaviour only in the most tenuous way. Beliefs and intentions are thought of as mental and, therefore, as private to the person whose beliefs and intentions they are; whereas bodily movements are physical and, therefore, publicly observable. Behaviour, it is supposed, is to be understood only by analysing it into its constituent components – beliefs, intentions and bodily movements – and understanding each of these in isolation. Only when this is done is the question of how they are related in behaviour raised, although with little prospect of a satisfactory answer. And knowledge of the behaviour of others can be gained, if at all, only by obtaining, independently, knowledge of each of its parts and uniting them by a separate process of synthesis.

There are two fundamental mistakes in this way of looking at things. The first is that of supposing that the mental and the physical are mutually exclusive, so that the same phenomenon cannot be both. This explains the Cartesian willingness to attribute to all mental phenomena a characteristic which is in fact possessed only by some, that of privacy. Some mental phenomena, such as dreams and unspoken thoughts, do not possess physical existence and, therefore, are private to the person whose dream or thought they are. Others, however, including not only behaviour but also thoughts which are given physical expression in being spoken or written down, do possess physical existence and, therefore, can be publicly observed.

Behaviour, then, can be observed because it involves bodily movements which possess physical existence. The second mistake is that of supposing that *all* that can be observed is the bodily movements involved in behaviour and not the behaviour itself. This is a consequence of supposing that behaviour is to be understood by analysing it into its constituent elements, each of which, in turn, can be understood without reference to the other elements involved. The bodily movements involved in behaviour are seen as bodily movements; and knowledge of the other elements in behaviour – the mental elements – is gained in some other way. The behaviour itself is then no more than a logical construction out of these separate elements and knowledge of it arrived at only by a process of synthesis.

This, however, is the reverse of the truth. It is only in special circumstances – for example, when a time-and-motion study is being made – that the bodily movements involved in behaviour are seen as bodily movements and, therefore, as detached from the behaviour of which they are a part. Behaviour is normally seen as behaviour and, therefore, as guided by beliefs and directed towards the achievement of ends. The ability to see it in this way is something which we normally take for granted; but it is in fact as sophisticated an achievement as the use of language. And it depends, like all observation, on possession of the relevant concepts.

vi

THE IDENTIFICATION OF BEHAVIOUR

Possession of behavioural concepts, then, is a necessary condition of seeing behaviour as behaviour and as behaviour of the relevant kind; for example, of seeing picking apples *as* picking apples. This leaves unanswered, however, the question of how we know which things are of a particular sort; that is, how an observer knows that what he is looking at is in fact picking apples, so that he is justified in seeing it in that way. In part the answer is that we rely on behavioural criteria. The movements of a person picking apples are not random but orderly and have clearly observable consequences: apples are moved from the tree to containers, to the storehouse and so on. This cannot be the complete answer, however, since two instances of behaviour may present the same appearance even though they differ in the intention involved and should not, therefore, be seen as of the same kind. For example, the intention in digging a hole in a churchyard is usually different from that in digging a hole in a road. Almost inevitably, however, the way in which these examples have been described makes it clear not only that they are different but also how an observer would know that they were different. Behaviour takes place in a context; and must be observed in that context if it is to be understood. The description of the examples, therefore, included a reference to their respective contexts, a churchyard and a road. These in turn locate the behaviour not only physically but also socially. An observer is normally already aware of the part which churches and churchyards, and road and supply cables, play in our social life. In the one case, therefore, the behaviour is seen as that of a gravedigger preparing a grave, in the other as a council workman uncovering pipes and cables. And in seeing it in this way an observer relies not just on what is currently before him but also on his knowledge of the context of the behaviour.

vii
THE DANGER OF MISUNDERSTANDING BEHAVIOUR

It might be thought that I have spent a great deal of time drawing attention to a danger, that of misunderstanding behaviour which, even if it is admitted, is unlikely to be encountered in practice. We can quite easily observe the behaviour of others; and mistakes, when they occur, are easily explained. The man digging a hole in the churchyard could, after all, have been searching for a gas leak. Nor is our ability to observe the behaviour of those around us surprising. Children acquire the concepts needed to do so from those around them in the normal course of growing up. It would not be easy to give a satisfactory philosophical account of how it is possible for them to do so. But the fact that they do so explains why the members of the same community tend to share the same concepts and, therefore, to make use of the same concepts in their observations and behaviour. Indeed, it is almost definitive of a community that this is so. It is not surprising, therefore, that the concepts used in the observation of behaviour normally coincide with the concepts used by the person whose behaviour is being observed.

There are, however, circumstances in which this coincidence cannot be taken for granted. The most striking examples occur when different and hitherto separate communities come into contact; for example, when the American frontiersmen encountered the native American tribes or when the first Australian settlers met the aboriginal inhabitants. At a superficial level their observations may have been accurate enough; but they often failed to achieve any real understanding of what they saw. In this century, social anthropologists such as Malinowski, Levy-Bruhl and Evans-Pritchard have made more systematic and careful attempts to understand primitive societies. In doing so, however, they have been in very real danger of interpreting what they saw in terms of their own Western concepts rather than finding out the meaning which the members of the society being studied attached to their behaviour themselves. The practice of consulting oracles before planting crops, for example, is easily misinterpreted as a piece of misguided technology.

It is worth asking, at this point, how a social anthropoligist goes about understanding and describing the ways of behaving which are typical of a society other than his own. Despite the considerable methodological difficulties, there is a very simple answer. He goes to the place where the members of that society live and lives amongst them for a considerable period of time. This answer is by no means trivial. It might be thought, for example, that first-hand observations were unnecessary and that reliance could be placed on the casual reports of travellers and traders whose primary business lay elsewhere. Or that the advantages of first-hand observation might be obtained without the inconvenience of travel by employing others to bring back specimens of the society, which could then be studied in comfort and convenience at home. That, after all, is a perfectly proper procedure when dealing with such things as soil samples and rock cores.

Reliance has been placed on both of these methods in the past; but they have fallen increasingly into disfavour. Casual reports from travellers are likely to be inaccurate; but, more important, they are bound to be superficial, since, in being fragmentary, they cannot relate the behaviour to the social context which gives it meaning. It is as though, in the example used earlier, we are told that a man is digging a hole but are not told anything else; and are then invited to say whether he is digging a grave, mending the road or, perhaps, doing something quite different. We could guess; but we would have been deprived of the information needed to arrive at a considered opinion. Reliance on specimens is equally unsatisfactory for the same basic reason. Although the idea of an anthropological zoo is obviously absurd, there are anthropological museums; for example, there is a collection of totem poles at the University of British Columbia. By any standard they are impressive in their scale and craftsmanship. But a student of West Coast Indians could not, from an examination of the totem poles themselves, discover their meaning or the part they played in the lives of the people who constructed them. It is true that in the case of prehistoric man all we have to go on is the archaeological record; but our understanding is correspondingly limited. An examination of Stonehenge, for example, however careful, cannot tell us what it was constructed for. And it would be pointless for a social anthropologist to put himself in a similarly disadvantaged position unnecessarily.

The danger of misundertanding is reduced if attention is confined to our own society. For the most part we can easily understand the behaviour of the people we meet in the normal course of living and working. But once we depart from that course, by chance or deliberate intent, we can no longer take our understanding of the behaviour of others for granted. For example, a non-believer in a church may fail to understand much of what he sees because he does not share the congregation's way of looking at things; and this may be so also in the case of a non-scientist in a laboratory, a visitor or patient in a hospital, and so on. Members of professions, as a matter of definition, possess knowledge and skills, attitudes and purposes and, generally, ways of looking at things which are not shared by the community at large. In their case also, therefore, there is a real danger of misunderstanding. In the case of education, this might take the form of a communication gap between, for example, parents and the schools which their children attend. Parent–teacher associations are, in part, a recognition of the possibility of such a gap and of the desirability of bridging it. In philosophy of education, also, there is a danger that the philosopher will try to impose his own conceptions of what education is or ought to be on to phenomena to which they do not belong. This is particularly likely to happen if education is thought of as having an unchanging nature or essence, to which only the philosopher has access and which only he can understand. Later, in section 4 of the following chapter, attention is drawn to the ambiguity of the question 'What is education?' and the danger of misunderstanding which attempts to answer it involve.

3
THE REALITY OF SOCIAL PHENOMENA

In section 6 of the previous chapter I said that the members of a profession see themselves, and are seen by others, as members of a profession. Being seen as a profession, therefore, is not something which follows, independently, on being a profession but is an essential part *of* being a profession. This feature of a profession is one which, to some extent, is shared by all social phenomena, although it has an additional dimension which will be considered in section 4.

Judged by the standards of physical phenomena, this feature of social phenomena is a very odd one. In their case, we suppose that they are what they are independently of what they are taken to be and, indeed, independently of whether anyone has any beliefs about them and of the content of the beliefs which anyone may happen to have about them. For example, whether Chimborazo is the highest peak in the Andes depends solely on the height of Chimborazo relative to that of other Andean peaks. It does not depend on its being seen in that or, indeed, in any other way. Chimborazo existed, presumably, long before there was anybody around to see it and certainly before anyone had a sufficiently unified conception of the geography of South America to think in terms of continental mountain ranges or knew how to measure the height of mountain peaks accurately. Whether Chimborazo is the highest peak in the Andes, therefore, is a straightforward question of fact, to be settled by making the relevant observations.

Social phenomena, however, possess a dimension, that of meaning, which physical phenomena lack. As pointed out in the previous section, they must be understood rather than, simply, observed; and they can be understood only if the concepts involved in them are grasped. Social phenomena consist primarily of things which people do; that is, make observations and behave in various ways. To grasp the concepts involved in them, therefore, is to realise how the person himself sees what he is doing. To fail to do so is to fail to identify the phenomena correctly, since how the person sees what he is doing is *part of* what he is doing, not something additional to it. Consequently the easiest and, in some ways, the most reliable way of finding out what someone is doing is to ask them.

The difference between physical and social reality becomes clearer if the conclusions summarised in the previous paragraph are expressed negatively. The positive conclusion was that a person seeing the highest peak in the Andes takes himself to be seeing the highest peak in the Andes. Conversely, however, a person who does not take himself to be seeing the highest peak in the Andes is not doing so; and similarly for behaviour. In other words, whereas physical phenomena are what they are independently of what they are taken to be, social phenomena depend for their reality on what they are taken to be. It does not follow without qualification that in all cases social phenomena are what they are taken to be. First, there is a perfectly ordinary sense in which it is possible for a person to think that he is seeing or doing something when he is not in fact doing so. For example, Stanley might have made a mistake in his calculations as a result of which he thought he was seeing the highest peak in the Andes when in fact he was seeing the second highest. Secondly, there is a sense in which it is possible for a person to see or do something without realising that that is what he is seeing or doing. Stanley saw Chimborazo as the highest peak in the Andes whereas Livingstone saw it only as Chimborazo. But if Chimborazo is in fact the highest peak in the Andes there is a sense in which Livingstone also saw the highest peak in the Andes when he saw Chimborazo, even though he did not realise that that was what he was seeing. In the case of behaviour, similarly, a farmer may think of what he is doing simply as picking apples and taking them to market, when in fact he is also contributing to the apple glut. There is a sense, therefore, in which what he is doing is contributing to the apple glut, even though that is not his intention and he does not realise that this is what he is doing. Indeed, it is not necessary for him to know what an apple glut is for it to be possible to describe his behaviour in that way.

There are many other examples of social phenomena which do not depend for their reality on what they are taken to be; perhaps the clearest is that of inflation. To avoid confusion, therefore, it is necessary to distinguish between descriptions of social phenomena at what might be called the ground-floor or phenomenological level, which allow them to be identified as social phenomena, and descriptions at higher levels. At the phenomenological level, social phenomena do depend for their reality on what they are taken to be. Once they are identified and described at this level, however, it is then possible for an observer to make further observations and offer other descriptions of them. In the nature of the case, descriptions at the ground-floor level must make use only of the concepts involved in the phenomena themselves. Descriptions at the higher level are not themselves subject to this restriction; but in order to be descriptions of social phenomena at all they must take for granted or include a description at the phenomenological or ground-floor level. For example, the possibility of saying that Livingstone saw the highest peak in the Andes, even though he did not know that that was what he was seeing, takes for granted the possibility of some description at the phenomenological level of what he saw, for example, 'Livingstone saw Chimborazo', and saying that Stanley mistakenly thought he saw the highest peak in the Andes takes for granted some description at the phenomenological level, such as Stanley saw Chimborazo as the highest peak in the Andes. Similarly, to say that what the farmer is doing is contributing to the apple glut is to assume he is doing something at the phenomenological level – i.e. marketing apples – in consequence of which the apple glut is increased. If the descriptions at the phenomenological level are eliminated altogether from the account, then there are no grounds for saying we are talking about social phenomena at all.

In relation to descriptions of social phenomena, therefore, one can make a distinction between participants' concepts and observers' concepts. An observer's description must employ participants' concepts but may also employ concepts which need not be available to the participants themselves. The farmer, for example, must have the concepts of apples and a market in apples; but need not have the concept of an apple glut. The terms 'observers' concepts' and 'participants' concepts' must, of course, be understood as relative to the social phenomena being observed. Since the observation of social phenomena is itself a social phenomenon, then what from the point of view of the original observation is an observer's concept would become, from the point of view of an observer of *that* observation, a participant's concept.

The difference between offering descriptions at the phenomenological and at higher levels reflects the difference between the social anthropologist and the sociologist. The problem facing a person studying a society other than his own is primarily that of understanding ways of looking at things and ways of behaving which differ from his own. His primary aim, therefore, is to describe that society at the phenomenological level; that is, to say things like 'Livingstone saw Chimborazo' rather than 'Livingstone saw the highest peak in the Andes' or 'The farmer is marketing his apples' rather than 'The farmer is contributing to the apple glut'. For the sociologist studying his own society, however, understanding the phenomena he is studying is normally unproblematic, since he is himself a member of that society. He is free, therefore, to make higher-level observations about them; that is, to say things like

'Livingstone saw the highest peak in the Andes' or 'The farmer is contributing to the apple glut'.

It is of course an oversimplification to characterise the difference between social anthropology and sociology in this way. Social anthropologists do make higher-level statements about the societies they study. They may, for example, describe their thought as pre-logical or their behaviour as irrational; or apply to them cultural concepts like pre-scientific, economic concepts like inflation, or Freudian concepts such as that of an Oedipus conflict. There is no *a priori* reason why they should not do so, provided they have first understood the society at the phenomenological level; although whether the statements they make are true is, of course, a further question. Similarly, sociologists can take for granted an understanding of their own society, provided that society is homogeneous in its outlook. There is no reason to suppose that this can be taken for granted, however, in a society sufficiently complex to include sociologists and other minority groups such as religious sects, social classes and so on. It follows from the account of a profession that the members of a profession, also, form a group only within and as part of a larger social whole or community; and that their characteristically professional way of looking at things is shared only to a limited extent by the rest of the community.

4

A PROFESSION AS A SOCIAL PHENOMENON

i

SOCIAL GROUPS AND SOCIAL ACTIVITIES

In the previous section I pointed out that social phenomena at the phenomenological level depend for their identity on what they are taken to be. Only after they have been identified and described at this level is it possible to observe and describe them at a higher level.

So far I have talked only about behaviour and the making of

observations, although I admitted earlier that, since they need not involve other people, neither would normally be thought of as social. Mountain peaks can be observed and apples picked in solitude. But the observations which others make and the ways in which they behave can themselves be observed. To observe them is to see others as like oneself in possessing the ability to make observations and behave in various ways; that is, to see them as people. Behaviour also may involve the recognition of others as people who can be expected to see and understand that behaviour and to respond to it through their own behaviour. People form groups, therefore, the members of which not only share ways of looking at things and behaving but also realise that they share them; they not only form groups but see themselves as forming groups.

Not every group which people form depends for its reality on being seen as a group by its members. For example, all the red-headed people in a town are members of the class of red-headed people who live in that town; but it is not necessary for them to think of themselves as members of that class in order to *be* members of that class. They might come to think of themselves as a group, however, if by some accident they all found themselves in the same room at the same time. In thinking of themselves as the class of red-headed people they would automatically form a second group, that of the people who saw themselves and each other as members of the class of red-headed people. This group would depend for its existence on being seen as a group by its members. Such a group, therefore, is a social phenomenon at the phenomenological level and will be referred to as a primary social group.

The group of red-headed people, as such, would not be of any special interest, even if they formed a primary social group as defined above. That they are able to see themselves in this or any other way, however, is a consequence of their self-consciousness and, indeed, of their shared self-consciousness. They could not see each other as red-headed unless they shared the same way of looking at things, at least to the extent of all possessing the concept of red-headedness. In the same way, Stanley and Livingstone may see Chimborazo in the same way – as the highest peak in the Andes – and may, therefore, come to realise that they do. Moreover, further dimensions might be added to their awareness. Stanley may realise not only that Livingstone sees things as he does but also that Livingstone realises that he, Stanley, is aware that this is so, and vice versa. Each, therefore, forms a mirror for the other's self-awareness. I will refer to this as reciprocal self-awareness.

There is a close connection, which was explored in section 2 (iii), between the way people see things and the way in which they behave; and there is no reason why this reciprocal self-awareness should not extend to behaviour. Let us suppose, for example, that Stanley and Livingstone share a common purpose, that of climbing the highest peak in the Andes, that each knows that they do and that each knows that the other knows. If both wanted to be the first person to climb that peak, then, with a little further reflection, they might come to see each other as rivals. If their desire was simply to climb it, however, then they might just as easily come to see each other as allies. They would then be in a position to form an expedition, the purpose of which would be the same as that of the individuals who were its members. In either case – whether they saw each other as rivals or as allies – the details of their behaviour would be modified to take into account the additional dimension which their situation now possessed, even though their primary purpose remained the same. Their situation, that is, their social situation, is changed by the way they see themselves and each other.

In the same way, the members of a profession make observations and behave in various ways as they go about their professional business. In being members of a profession they are not simply isolated individuals pursuing their own purposes without regard for one another. They are members of a group each of whom is aware that he is a member of that group and of the professional purposes which he shares with other members of that group; and aware, also, that other members of the group are aware of his awareness. This reciprocal self-awareness is part of what a profession is – of the social reality itself – and not something external to it. The observations and behaviour of its members, which together constitute the professional activity of the group, are modified by it and cannot be fully understood in isolation from it.

ii
A PROFESSION AS A SOCIAL PHENOMENON

In the previous section I pointed out that social phenomena at the phenomenological level depend for their reality on being seen as what they are; and earlier in this section I introduced primary social groups as a kind of social phenomenon at the phenomenological level in addition to observations and behaviour.

A profession is a social phenomenon in that its members see themselves as members of a social group. In the case of a profession, however, it is not sufficient for its members to see themselves as a profession. They must also be recognised as a profession by the rest of the community. Public recognition is something additional to the other grounds on which it might be claimed and does not follow automatically on their satisfaction. It is possible for a group of people to satisfy all the requirements to which attention was drawn earlier and, therefore, have every reason to claim to be recognised as a profession, without being recognised as a profession by the rest of the community. And, without that recognition, they will not *be* a profession.

There is, therefore, a further sense in which a profession depends for its reality on being seen as what it is. The nature of, and need for, this further requirement can be seen more easily if a profession is compared with a primary social group to which it does not apply, for example the red-headed people living in the same town who, by some accident, come to think of themselves as a group. The analogy can be strenghtened by supposing that their perception of themselves as a group, initially wholly passive, leads to practical social activities. Whether the rest of the people living in the town see them as a social group will then depend, straightforwardly, on the nature of those activities. For example, if they take to parading through the streets carrying banners bearing the legend 'The League of Red-headed Men', or set up a clubhouse similarly captioned, they will obviously draw attention to themselves and their group identity will be recognised. On the other hand, their activities may be criminal, in which case they will take care to keep them secret; or they may seek power and influence by setting up a secret network of mutual patronage. Or, again, their activities may be both innocuous and unobtrusive, in which case it will be a matter of chance whether their existence is noticed. Recognition by the rest of the townspeople, therefore, may be seen by the League of Red-headed Men as desirable, undesirable or a matter of indifference; but its *being* the League of Red-headed Men will not depend on such recognition.

In the case of a profession, however, the nature of its activities is such that its members must regard recognition as desirable. They think that they have something of value to offer to the community; and in recognising them as a profession the community is agreeing that this is so. It follows that the community will be willing to pay for the profession's services and will accord its members social status and prestige. But this is not the main point. Professional purposes, as such, are concerned not with the interest of those whose purposes they are but with the interests of others. This ideal of service, the possibility of which was defended in section 1, is central to the idea of a profession. The members of a profession regard service to the community as an end in itself, not simply as a means to other things such as money and status. In other words, they think that they have something of *intrinsic* value to offer to the community; and they want the community to benefit from their activities, not simply to benefit from them themselves. They must, therefore, want to be allowed to provide their services to the community; and public recognition is, in effect, their licence to do so. It is at the same time a recognition of their specialised knowledge and skills and their willingness to use them to the best of their ability without any form of external supervision or duress. Consequently they themselves are seen as the people best qualified and motivated to supervise their own professional activities.

A profession cannot, therefore, function as a profession unless it is recognised as such by the rest of the community, since recognition brings with it certain consequences which are essential to its functioning. Without recognition it would be like a bodily organ, such as a heart or kidney, which in itself is sound but which is rejected by the body into which it has been transplanted. The body needs the organ and the organ is perfectly capable of serving the body provided it is allowed to do so. But it cannot function as a bodily organ if it is rejected. There is, of course, an explanation of the body's rejection of a transplanted organ; and there may also be an explanation of a community's refusal to recognise a profession. But whatever the explanation, the consequence is the same. The profession or organ cannot function as a profession or organ and, since it is in part identified as what it is by reference to its function, cannot be a profession or organ. The League of Red-headed Men, on the other hand, need make no positive contribution to the life of the community in order to be what it is. It would not, therefore, cease to be what it is if it were frustrated in any attempts which it might make to contribute to the life of the community.

iii
PUBLIC RECOGNITION

There is now a further reason why the question whether a particular group of people form a profession is not, straightforwardly, a question of fact to be settled by consulting the evidence. In admitting a new group of people to the professional club the community is not simply making a decision on a matter of fact but is adopting a new attitude to them. Indeed, it is the favourable attitude itself, rather than possible grounds for it, which most people associate with the idea of a profession.

In the previous chapter I tried to give an account of the sort of grounds on which a group of people might be recognised as a profession and, therefore, on which a favourable attitude to them might rationally be based. At first sight it might seem as though, given the satisfaction of those grounds, the favourable attitude would follow automatically. Some explanation of why this is not so, therefore, is required.

(a) *Beliefs and attitudes.* What counts as evidence for a belief is laid down by the nature of the belief itself; to accept the evidence whilst rejecting the belief would, therefore, be irrational. It cannot be denied that people are often irrational. For example, a child promised a picnic at the seaside provided the weather is suitable may refuse to accept gathering storm clouds as evidence of rain to come. Anybody who wishes to be rational, however, cannot accept the evidence for a belief whilst rejecting the belief itself.

In general, however, what counts as grounds for holding an attitude is not laid down by the nature of the attitude in the same way. For example, one child may be favourably disposed towards the idea of a trip to the seaside because the weather is fine and sunny, whereas its sibling may prefer to go when there is a prospect of a storm. It is true that most people share the former attitude, so that the beaches become crowded when the weather is fine. But we would not say that anyone who held the latter attitude was irrational, only that their tastes were unusual.

The connection, then, between attitudes and the grounds for them is different from that between beliefs and the evidence for them. It is possible for two people to agree as to the facts whilst at the same time adopting different attitudes to those facts, 'possible' here meaning 'logically possible'. In practice, however, it may be extremely difficult for them to do so. This is because many of the words in our language are both descriptive and evaluative; in using them to describe, therefore, we are automatically committed to the attitudes which they incorporate. For example, the word 'murder' does not just mean 'killing' but 'wrongful killing'. We can avoid this commitment, however, by using words which are descriptive only or which have different evaluative meaning. Instead of 'murdered', for example, we could simply say 'killed', 'killed in self-defence' or 'executed'. It has been argued that in some cases – the favourite examples being 'rude' and 'courageous' – we cannot avoid commitment to the appropriate attitude in this way. We could, it is true, describe the behaviour concerned in purely descriptive terms, avoiding words like 'rude' or 'courageous' and confining ourselves to what the person actually did. Having done so, however, we could not, it is argued, then deny that the behaviour was rude or courageous without inconsistency.

If this argument were correct and applied to the word 'profession' it would follow that there could not be a gap between satisfaction of the grounds on which recognition as a profession might be rationally based and recognition itself. I can see no reason, however, why two people should not agree as to the facts about a group claiming recognition as a profession whilst at the same time adopting different attitudes to them and, therefore, disagreeing about whether that claim should be accepted. They might certainly *describe* each other as unreasonable; but I cannot see how there could be any objective grounds for either attitude to be condemned as irrational.

Attitudes, therefore, cannot be rational or irrational in the way in which beliefs can. Nevertheless there is a sense in which there may be grounds on which recognition as a profession might be rationally based. First, it must be based on beliefs about the facts of the case which are themselves rational in being based on the relevant evidence. Secondly, the beliefs must constitute *reasons* for the recognition in the sense that other groups of people who are similar in the relevant respects are treated in the same way. The grounds offered must be the kind of grounds which are generally accepted and required to be accepted by the conventions of the community concerned. Thus the word 'unreasonable' is sometimes used to describe people whose attitudes are unacceptable by generally accepted standards, for example people who are rude without provocation or who insist on having more than their fair share of cake or some other desirable good according to a generally accepted convention. And, thirdly, there must be some intelligible connection between the facts on which recognition is based and the consequences which follow from it. For example, the fact that a group of people possess special knowledge and skills and, without any form of external pressure, are willing to use them to the best of their ability for the advantage of the community is in an obvious sense a reasonable ground for according that group of people a large measure of autonomy in the conduct of their professional affairs. But rational grounds in this sense do not compel acceptance in the way in which rational grounds for holding beliefs do.

(b) *Descriptive and emotive meaning.* I have already mentioned the fact that beliefs are not always rational. People often believe what they want to believe or what they are persistently told to believe. Indeed, if they are persistently told what they want to believe they are likely to believe it even if it is directly contrary to the evidence. If the magic mirror on the wall always tells its owner that she is the fairest of them all, she is likely to believe it however clear the evidence to the contrary provided by her own reflection.

In the case of attitudes, the scope for rationality is less than in the case of beliefs and the scope for manipulating them correspondingly greater. Moreover, the favourable attitude involved in recognition as a profession brings with it obvious advantages, including increased social status, reward and autonomy. These consequences are desirable even if recognition is not based on the rational grounds to which I have drawn attention. In these circumstances, therefore, some will lay claim to and receive privileges which they do not deserve whilst the just claims of others are ignored.

The facts to which I have just drawn attention have taken their toll on the meaning of the word 'profession', tending to strip it of cognitive or descriptive meaning and leaving only its emotive meaning. Professor Charles L. Stevenson made an important contribution to philosophy and, more generally, rationality in public debate, by drawing attention to the possibility of changes of meaning of this sort. The standard example is that of the word 'democracy', which can be used informatively to refer either to certain sorts of political institutions, for example those which make use of voting procedures, or to the ideals by reference to which such institutions are justified, for example the ideal of the equal worth and dignity of men. It is also increasingly used, however, simply to refer to any form or institution of government of which the speaker approves and wishes others to approve. Its use solely to influence attitudes, without regard to its original descriptive meaning, constitutes an impoverishment of language, making it impossible to say that one is in favour of democracy without uttering a trivial tautology. To say that the United States or the U.S.S.R. is a democracy becomes simply an expression of approval of the one or the other; it gives no indication of the kind of evidence which would count for or against its being a democracy and, therefore, which would support or undermine such a favourable attitude to it.

Part of my purpose in chapter two was to resist the tendency to trivialise the word 'profession' in the same way, if necessary by stipulating a clear descriptive meaning for it. Given such a meaning, it is then possible to claim that teaching is a profession; and to be able to mean by it not simply that the speaker has an attitude of approval towards teachers but that he has good grounds for that attitude.

I do not wish to give the impression that I am against the use of persuasive techniques as such. The mere presentation of the grounds for claiming that teaching is a profession, however adequate, may by itself fail to overcome the inertia of traditional social attitudes. If so, the use of techniques of persuasion would be both necessary and justified. The fact that they are often used improperly is no reason why proper use should not be made of them.

5
IS TEACHING A PROFESSION?

Following the account of a profession in chapter two, I went on to point out that a profession is a social phenomenon; and in this chapter have tried to give an account of the nature of social phenomena. Social phenomena, it was pointed out, possess a dimension of meaning; consequently they must be understood rather than straightforwardly observed. And there is a corresponding danger that they may be misunderstood. Moreover, a profession is a complex kind of social phenomenon. As in the case of other primary social groups, it owes its existence to the perception by its members of their membership and, additionally, to its recognition as a profession by the rest of the community. On speaking of a group of people as forming a profession, therefore, we are speaking about how they see themselves and are seen by others.

Despite these difficulties and complexities, in the final analysis it is a question of fact whether a group of people such as teachers form a profession and, as such, outside the province of philosophy. Nevertheless something can be said, in a general way, about the question whether teaching is a profession.

(a) *No general answer* can be given to the question whether teaching, or, for that matter, medicine, is a profession. It cannot be answered *a priori* by an analysis of the word 'teaching'. Nor, perhaps less obvious, can it be settled by consulting the facts, since the relevant facts vary from time to time and from place to place. But more specific questions about whether particular groups of people such as teachers in England and Wales in the nineteenth century formed a profession can be answered by making the appropriate enquiries.

(b) *No clear answer* to any such question is to be expected, since there are a number of criteria to be satisfied, and a group of people may satisfy some without satisfying others. For example, nurses may score high on responsibility and idealism but low, relative to doctors, on pay and knowledge and skill. Even if there is agreement on the basic criteria to be applied, therefore, there is still room for disagreement on the relative weight to be attached to each.

(c) *Complexity*. The relevant facts are likely to be extremely complex and difficult to establish. For example, no short, simple answer to the question 'Are teachers relatively well paid?' is to be expected. The answer will depend partly on who they are being compared with; they may be paid well compared with one group and badly when compared with another. Apart from the problem of establishing a relevant standard, the question of how much teachers are in fact paid is itself extremely complex. The salary paid to any one teacher will depend on a variety of factors, including age, experience, qualifications, responsibility, scale for the appropriate institution, and so on. Comparisons with similar groups are bound to be complex, therefore.

(d) *Inaccessibility*. Questions like 'How far are teachers motivated by an ideal of service to the community?' are even more difficult to answer. I argued earlier that the intentions and purposes on which people act are not in principle unobservable; nevertheless they are difficult to observe with any assurance of reliability.

I have said enough to show that the practical difficulties involved in saying whether a particular group of people form a profession are very great. Even if they are not insuperable, therefore, no simple yes-or-no answer is to be expected.

This conclusion, inconclusive though it is, has consequences for the line of enquiry I am pursuing. Although I have tried to give an account which is highly general in character, the group of people in whom I am particularly interested is that of teachers in our own society today. But, it might be argued, they do not, as a matter of fact, form a profession; the suggestion that they do is, perhaps, idealistic, but it is also highly unrealistic. And, that being so, the present enquiry lacks point. It might be relevant to some group of groups of teachers at some other place or time but it is not relevant to teaching as we know it. In anticipation of this objection, there are a number of points which I would like to make. First, in the absence of definite evidence one way or the other, there is scope for difference of opinion about the matter; and my opinion, for what it is worth, is that teaching is a profession. Secondly, since the question of fact remains unanswered, any philosophy of education which ignores the possibility that teaching is a profession is equally vulnerable, although for the opposite reason. Thirdly, if teaching is not a profession, then I think that that is a pity. And it is legitimate to hope that, simply through the question's being raised, teachers may be led to consider how far their practice conforms to the criteria put forward (inevitably a matter of degree) and whether it is desirable that it should.

CHAPTER THREE: NOTES AND REFERENCES

1. I have had no particular exponent of psychological hedonism in mind in this section. It is, however, an extremely common view among philosophers and non-philosophers alike. A version of it is put forward in the story of Gyges' ring in Book II of Plato's *Republic*, where it is suggested that any man who could become invisible by wearing a ring would, in Plato's words, 'go to the market place and fearlessly help himself to anything he wanted, enter houses and sleep with any women he chose, set prisoners free and kill men at his pleasure, and in a word go about among men with the powers of a god' (p. 44 in the Oxford edition of the *Republic*, edited by F. M. Cornford). This is taken to show that men act justly only for fear of the consequences of acting unjustly. As mentioned in the note to section 4 of the previous chapter, Jeremy Bentham appears to have shared this view; hence his view of law as the science of intimidation.

2. Within philosophy, attention was drawn to the meaningfulness of behaviour by Professor Peter Winch's book *The Idea of a Social Science*. I do not accept Winch's view, based on the private language argument, that all meaningful behaviour is necessarily social. I see no reason why the behaviour of isolated animals should not be meaningful.

I have referred to the view of behaviour criticised in (v) as Cartesian. The relevant features of Descartes's conception of the mental, however, were also shared by Locke and other empiricists. In combination with the empiricist atomistic metaphysic it leads to a search for the basic units or atoms of behaviour from which more complex behaviours are supposed to be constructed. For Descartes's view of the mind see his *Discourse on Method*, especially Part IV, and *Meditations on the First Philosophy*, especially Meditation II, and, for Locke's, Book I of his *Enquiry concerning Human Understanding*. A lot of attention has been paid recently to the relation between behaviour and bodily movement, for example in Professor A. I. Meldon's *Free Action*.

The problem raised by the need to understand behaviour and the consequent possibility of misunderstanding it is discussed in *Rationality*, edited by Bryan R. Wilson.

3. Following the argument of the previous section, I suggest in the text that social phenomena depend for their reality on what they are taken to be. It is a consequence of this view that social concepts – that is, concepts used to describe social phenomena at the phenomenological level – cannot be applied retrospectively. For example, mangrove swamps existed before there were men to describe them; but can now be retrospectively described as mangrove swamps existing at such-and-such a time in the past by modern geologists. By contrast, Boy Scouts could not have existed prior to the introduction of the idea of a Boy Scout with the inception of the Boy Scout movement by Lord Baden-Powell. No matter what historians discover about the behaviour of boys prior to that time, it cannot provide grounds for describing them as Boy Scouts. A similar point is made by Winch on p. 125 of *The Idea of a Social Science*: 'There existed electrical storms and thunder long before there were human beings to form concepts of them or establish that there was any connection between them. But it does not make sense to suppose that human beings might have been issuing commands and obeying them before they came to form the concept of a command and obedience.'

4.(i) The concept of a person implicit in this section is that of one who has the concept of himself as and as seen by others as a person; it is, therefore, a concept of persons as necessarily social. (This definition needs to be elaborated, of course, in such a way as to avoid circularity.) It is therefore opposed to the Cartesian view that a person can be a person, and essentially complete as a person, without knowing whether other persons exist or without being socially related to them.

4.(iii)(a) The view I have in mind in discussing the concepts of rudeness and courage is that called descriptivism or neo-naturalism put forward, in particular, by Mrs Foot. In 'Moral beliefs' (*Proceedings of the Aristotelian Society*, LIX, 1958), for example, she says that 'It is not obvious what someone would mean if he said that temperance or courage were not good qualities, and this is not because of the "praising" sense of these *words*, but because of the things that courage and temperance are' (p. 208 in *The Is/Ought Question*, edited by W. D. Hudson).

Professor R. M. Hare's books *The Language of Morals* and *Freedom and Reason* are obviously relevant to the position adopted in this section. The feature of Hare's moral philosophy which I find unacceptable is its consistent individualism and consequent failure to recognise the importance of the idea of a moral community. On his view it is a contingent psychological matter that, 'fanatics' on one side, we all universalise more or less the same moral judgements.

4.(iii)(b) In 'Persuasive definitions' (*Mind*, 1937) Stevenson defines a persuasive definition as 'one which gives a new conceptual meaning to a familiar word without substantially changing its emotive meaning, and which is used with the conscious or unconscious purpose of changing, by this means, the direction of people's interests' (p. 32 in *Facts and Values*).

Professor Scheffler introduces the idea of programmatic definitions in *The Language of Education* which in changing the meanings of words are also intended to influence policy. The claim that teaching should be described as a profession, for example, is not simply a claim that teachers should be described but also treated in a new way. (The example is Scheffler's own.)

Codes of professional conduct

1
A CODE AS A SYSTEM OF RULES

i
RULES

In this chapter I want to consider the idea of a code of professional conduct, showing how it arises out of and mirrors the idea of a profession itself. I will try also to indicate the sort of content which it might be expected to have.

I would like to begin by considering the idea of a code as such and go on in the next section to compare a professional with a legal or moral code. There are, of course, fundamental disagreements in philosophy about the nature of law and morality and the relation between them. Nevertheless all three – professional, legal and moral codes – may be thought of as systems of rules which function as guides to behaviour and, therefore, create the possibility of stable social relations within a stable social order. I will take it, therefore, that 'code' is simply a synonym for 'system of rules'; its use serves primarily to remind us that we are dealing with a system of rules rather than with isolated individual rules. This interpretation is consistent with its more specialised use in the legal context, where to codify is to systematise a body of law which has been enacted piecemeal over a period of time. To codify, then, is to tidy up; and a code is simply a system of rules.

The philosophical questions which arise, if this approach is followed, concern the nature of rules and the way they are related to form a system. Rules are abstract entities in the sense that they can be identified only indirectly through the behaviour of individuals, including their behaviour towards one another, rather than directly, 'behaviour' being understood in the sense indicated in (iii) and (iv) of section 2 of the previous chapter. It follows from the account given there that the ways of behaving open to a person are limited not only by the physical movements which his body is capable of making but also by the concepts available to him. As pointed out earlier, children acquire concepts from those around them in the normal course of growing up in a particular community. Indeed, it is almost a matter of definition that the members of the same community share the same concepts and, therefore, share also the same ways of looking at things and behaving. The behaviour of the members of a community will, therefore, form patterns. But not all the patterns of group behaviour which can be observed will be due to the existence of a rule: the members of the group may simply share a habit of behaving in that way. A distinction must be made, therefore, between group habits and social rules.

Group habits will be considered first. A way of behaving may be open to a person, in the sense that he is physically able and knows what it would be like to behave in that way, without his actually behaving in that way. Members of the same community, however, tend to find themselves in similar circumstances and to react to them in similar ways. For example, the members of a village community may work in the fields during the heat of the day and so need to protect themselves from the sun; and wearing a hat may be a way of behaving which is open to them in order to do so. Each, therefore, has a reason for wearing a hat, since each has the same need to protect himself. Consequently most of them will wear hats most of the time when working in the fields; and the hats they wear are likely to be similar in being made from the same local materials and in the same traditional manner. The situation could be described, therefore, by saying that they are in the habit of wearing a hat when working in the fields, or that they do so usually or as a rule. There is no reason, however, why all of them should do so or why any of them should do so all the time. Some of them may suffer from the effects of the sun less than others, the sun may be less strong at some times of the day or year, and so on. Consequently most of them will have a reason for wearing a hat most of the time and, therefore, will do so; but some may occasionally, or even always, have no such reason and accordingly will not do so. In other words, each does what each, individually, has a reason to do or not to do; but since their circumstances are similar their behaviour will tend to converge.

A group habit such as I have described does not, however, amount to a social rule. Although the villagers do, as a rule, wear hats when working in the fields, there is no rule which requires them to do so. A rule discriminates amongst the ways of behaving which are open to a person, leaving some to the discretion of the individual but requiring or forbidding others. It does not, however, *make* him behave in the required way; it is still open to him, in the sense indicated earlier, to behave in the way forbidden or to neglect to behave in the way required by the rule. In order to fulfil its function of discriminating amongst possible ways of behaving, therefore, the rule must somehow bring it about that the individual behaves differently from the way in which he would have behaved in its absence.

Since rules can be and often are broken, they are not completely successful in achieving this result; and in so far as they are, there is no one way in which they do so. Among those whose behaviour conforms, at least externally, to the norm, a distinction must be made between what I will call normal, rule-abiding persons on the one hand and rule-breakers and potential rule-breakers on the other. The normal, rule-abiding person has a reason, simply in being a member of the social group to whom the rule applies, for behaving in the way required by it; following a rule is simply a matter of behaving in the required way as a matter of course. The disposition to do so must be acquired at some stage, since the content of rules differs from one social group to another; and this involves both learning the content of the rule and acquiring the relevant motivation. Both are acquired by a process of learning from members of the social group who already possess them. In the case of a village community, they would be acquired through face-to-face contacts with parents, other adults and older children. In the case of a profession they are acquired as an important part of professional training and, thereafter, reinforced by the influence and example of other practitioners.

So far little has been said to distinguish social rules from group habits. I have introduced a new way of talking, saying that rules require or forbid certain ways of behaving; but I have also said that a rule does not compel obedience. The normal, rule-abiding person simply behaves in the required way as a matter of course because, as a result of his upbringing, he has a reason for behaving in that way. There is little difference so far, therefore, between following a rule and conforming to a group habit. In both cases, most members of the social group will behave as the rule requires or conform to the group habit; and in both cases, in the nature of the case, there may be a minority who fail to do so. Although, therefore, the only way to begin to understand the nature of social rules is by focusing attention on the normal, rule-abiding person, for a fuller understanding it is necessary to consider those who fail or are inclined to fail to abide by them.

I said earlier that, in the case of a group habit, there was no reason why all the members of the social group should conform to the habit or why any of them should do so all the time. In that case, therefore, it was necessary only to point out that conformity need not be universal. In the case of a social rule, however, the behaviour is required from all those to whom the rule applies and on all relevant occasions. Something needs to be added, therefore, about the position of the second group mentioned earlier, those who break or are inclined to break the rules and, therefore, who fail, more or less frequently, to behave in the required way.

The normal, rule-abiding person has a reason not only for behaving in the way required by a rule but also for seeing that others do so. Rules are seen as impersonal standards which all are required to obey, whether they want to or not, in contrast to group habits, which an individual can discard at will. To accept a rule is to see others as like oneself in being bound by the same rule and to see others as seeing oneself in the same way. The possibility of rule-following, therefore, depends on reciprocal self-awareness between those to whom the rule applies. To accept a rule, therefore, is not simply a matter of following it oneself but also of expecting and, indeed, requiring others to do so also. Consequently the failure of an individual to do so is likely to produce an adverse reaction from others. There are important differences between the reasons for such failures; between, that is, first, ignorance of what the rule requires and, secondly, unwillingness to do what it requires. Accordingly, reactions to breaches of rules from those who accept them as a general standard can be divided into two kinds.

(a) *Ignorance.* They will try to remove the ignorance if the rule seems to have been broken unintentionally in ignorance of its existence. Their action need not take the form of an explicit recital of the rule. It is more likely to take that of a simple act of correction or a stricter, less ambiguous model in their own behaviour.

(b) *Wilful breaches of rules.* On the other hand, if the rule appears to have been broken intentionally, they will try to provide the rule-breaker with a reason for obeying the rule. Ideally this would be the reason which the rule-abiding person has himself; in other words, attempts would be made to educate or, in the case of adults, reform or re-educate, the rule-breaker. Failing this, however – and there is every reason to expect it to fail when directed towards those who have already had every opportunity to acquire the appropriate motivation – reliance must be placed on forms of motivation which the rule-breaking person already possesses. In other words, sanctions must be applied to rule-breakers, the prospect of which so changes their situation that, on balance, they no longer want to break the rule.

I have said at the beginning of this section that rules function as guides to behaviour; and it is now possible to see more clearly how they are able to perform this function. So far as the normal, rule-abiding person is concerned, the guidance is self-guidance; it consists simply in having a reason for behaving in the way required by the rule. So far as the child or initiate is concerned, it consists in the example and influence of those already familiar with and committed to the way of life or activity concerned, that is, of the normal, rule-abiding members of the social group or existing practitioners of the activity. So far as the potential rule-breaker is concerned, the guidance is provided by others through their reactions or anticipated reactions to breaches of the rule. It is still rational guidance in the sense that it takes the form of providing a reason for obeying the rule, although not the standard reason which the rule-abiding person has. From the point of view of the rule-breaker, therefore, the rule is seen as possessing an independent existence and properties of its own; it is part of the external situation which must be taken into account in making plans and decisions. The point of view of the rule-breaker, however, is misleading as to the real nature of rules. The operation of a rule may be revealed by his activities and the reactions which they provoke; but he contributes nothing to its existence. Rules, like other social phenomena, depend for their reality on what they are taken to be; and it is the normal, rule-abiding person who sees them as impersonal standards which all are required to obey.

In the preceding paragraphs I have tried to distinguish between group habits and social rules and to give an account of what is being asserted when a rule is said to exist. The relevance of the distinction between group habits and social rules to an understanding of the nature of a profession may not be immediately obvious. The point is that the members of a profession may share certain habits – for example, City gents wear bowler hats and carry rolled umbrellas when travelling to work – without there being any rule requiring them to do so. It is not essential to their being, say, merchant bankers that they do so. Their doing so is not required by their being members of the banking profession, nor does it in any way make them members of that profession. On the other hand, an understanding of the social rules which make up the banker's code of professional conduct is essential to an understanding of what the banking profession is; and similarly for other professions.

ii

SYSTEMS OF RULES

So far I have said nothing about the way rules are related to each other to form a system. It is, however, extremely misleading to speak as though a rule could exist as a self-sufficient, discrete entity independently of a system of rules. It makes no sense, for example, to suppose that the offside rule in football could exist outside the context of the other rules which together constitute the game of football. It makes even less sense to suppose that parts of an independently viable way of life such as that of an isolated village community can be meaningfully isolated from the life of which they are a part. We do isolate parts of a game such as football or of the life of a village community for purposes of discussion; but such discussions take for granted a knowledge of the game or way of life from which the part is abstracted. This point is connected with that made earlier (in section 2(iv) of the previous chapter) about the need to understand behaviour if it is to be identified correctly and, therefore, if it is to be possible to observe it; and about the need to relate it to its context, especially its social context, if it is to be understood. And what has been said here about individual rules applies *a fortiori* to the behaviour of individuals on the occasions on which they follow or break rules, react to the behaviour of others in breaking them or react in turn to the reactions of others to their own infringements of rules.

The conclusion that rules must be thought of as parts of systems of rules is not surprising in view of the account of rules in (i) above. In that account, importance was attached to normal rule-followers and their influence on potential rule-breakers. So far as their own behaviour is concerned, however, following a rule is simply behaving in the required way as a matter of course. They have a reason for behaving in that way which, in all normal circumstances, take priority over any reason they may have for behaving differently. What this amounts to saying is that they behave as they do not because of any external pressures which are brought to bear upon them but because they are the sort of person they are. In so far, therefore, as people's personalities are integrated, forming coherent wholes, it is to be expected that the patterns of group behaviour which are constructed out of their permanent dispositions to behave in certain ways should display a similar integration and coherence. Moreover, this tendency is reinforced by their reactions to others who, although sharing the advantages of social life, fail to accept its obligations. To put it another way, those who follow the same rules share purposes which relate not to private, separate lives but to lives lived with others. To live with others, in this sense, is not necessarily to live with them physically: it is to share and to be conscious of sharing purposes to which importance is attached and, therefore, to which priority is given; and to accept, and to expect others to accept, responsibility for their achievement. Rules, in other words, are a kind of social mechanism or device which allow a community or social group to achieve the purposes which its members, as members, share; and those purposes, in turn, give point to the rules.

To talk about a system of rules is simply a convenient but abstract way of talking about a social group and, therefore, about the way the members of the group see themselves and their behaviour, and each other's behaviour. As was argued in section 4(i) of the previous chapter, the members of a social group see themselves and each other as members of that group; and each is aware, also, of being perceived as a member by the rest. Each therefore sees himself as bound by, and expects others to conform to, the behavioural norms of the group. A system of rules, therefore, has the same sort of unity and identity as a social group, deriving, ultimately, from its overall purpose. This can vary in degree of self-consciousness and vitality, but it should be especially marked in the case of a profession.

2
SOME WAYS IN WHICH SYSTEMS OF RULES DIFFER

In the previous section I considered the idea of a code of conduct, or system of rules, as such. Legal, moral and professional codes are similar in that they share the basic features of any such system; but there are also important respects in which they differ. In this section I will draw attention to a number of ways in which systems of rules might differ, under the headings of scope and content, authoritative statement, formal legislation, enforcement and criticism and change.

i
SCOPE AND CONTENT

Generally speaking, moral and legal codes apply to everyone and may relate to any aspect of their lives. Professional codes, on the other hand, apply only to the members of the relevant profession when acting in their professional capacity. Although intuitively obvious, this contrast is not as helpful as it seems, since 'everyone' here means 'every member of the relevant moral and legal community'. So far as content is concerned, however, the contrast may be more helpful. Attempts to define morality in terms of its content (leaving on one side the popular identification of morality, or rather immorality, with sex) tend to rely on extremely broad notions such as happiness, needs, interests or welfare, which in turn lack content. Similarly, although all legal systems include provisions designed to protect persons and property, they also deal with an endless variety of other matters. On the other hand, the sphere of activity of a profession is limited by its connection with specialised knowledge and skills. A code of professional conduct, therefore, may be expected to concern itself with the proper use of that knowledge and skill in order to achieve most effectively the professional purposes which the members of the profession share. The content of a professional code will be considered, therefore, in section 3.

The next three features, authoritative statement, formal legislation and enforcement are intimately connected. So far as possible, however, I will try to deal with them in turn.

ii

AUTHORITATIVE STATEMENT

All social rules possess some content, forbidding or requiring certain sorts of behaviour. There must, therefore, be some way in which that content is made known to those to whom the rules apply. The most basic method of doing so has already been discussed; it is that provided by the example of rule-abiding persons together with simple acts of correction when the child or initiate fails to follow the example correctly.

An alternative method, which is used typically by the law, is that of explicit statement. Such statements may be made orally, but there are obvious advantages in making them in writing. In either case, the person or body of persons making the statement must be consciously aware of the rule as a rule; this method, therefore, requires a degree of self-awareness which the simpler method does not and, in that sense, is more sophisticated. Those to whom the rule is to be communicated, also, must have some way of recognising such statements as statements of social rules which create genuine obligations. The most obvious way of doing so is by reference to their source; a parent or experienced member of a profession, for example, can reasonably be expected to know what the rules of the social group or profession are. Indeed, any rule-abiding member of a social group is an authority in this sense on what the rules of that group are.

iii
FORMAL LEGISLATION

Certain bodies, such as Parliament and local authorities, possess legislative powers; and in exercising them they are clearly not communicating the content of an existing rule but bringing a new one into existence. It has been suggested, therefore, that their official utterances are more accurately thought of as orders or commands rather than as statements, although they also provide the most authoritative account of what the law is. Legislative power is not confined to governments; there is no reason, for example, why the League of Red-headed Men should not have set up a committee to draw up rules to be observed by its members. Nor is there any reason why the members of a profession should not appoint a committee to draw up a code of conduct for the behaviour of the profession as a whole. And if they did so, then the rules which resulted would be legal rules in the sense of being the produce of legislation.

Legal rules are normally thought of, however, as those laid down and enforced by a lawful government. This has led to the view, associated particularly with Hobbes, that a legal rule is no more than the word of the person or body of persons possessing sovereign authority. If this view were correct it would clearly undermine the account of rules given in the previous section, which was intended as a general account of the most basic features of rules. The intention in this section is to draw attention to dimensions along which systems of rules, all sharing these basic features, might vary. I will try, therefore, to show that the Hobbesian view, although it does draw attention to ways in which legal differ from other systems of rules, is incomplete unless the account contained in the previous section is added to it.

Hobbes's account is incomplete without some account of what makes an authority a proper authority. His answer is that the authority of the sovereign, or lawful government, is derived from its ability to enforce its commands, that is, from its power. This is open to the objection that it reduces a moral concept, that of authority, to a non-moral concept, that of power, although Hobbes could legitimately claim that this is question-begging. More important, Hobbes's answer reverses the true order of things. A sovereign, or lawful government, does have power: it would not be a lawful government without it. But its power is derived from its authority, not vice versa. A lawful government has power *because* its commands are accepted; its commands are not accepted, at least in the final analysis, because it has power. And Hobbes is unable, within the limits set by his materialist presuppositions, to say why its commands are accepted.

A lawful government (and any lesser law-making body) is a social phenomenon and cannot be understood if thought of as, or as like, a physical phenomenon. Social phenomena, unlike physical ones, depend for their reality on what they are taken to be. A government which is seen as a lawful government will, in general, have its commands, edicts and decrees obeyed; it has authority because it is seen as having authority, and has power because it has authority. What brings a legal rule into existence, therefore, is not so much its expression but its acceptance by those to whom it applies; that is, its being seen as an impersonal standard set up by a proper authority. To put it in the terms used by Professor Hart in *The Concept of Law*, the primary rules laid down by a law-making body are accepted because a secondary rule conferring upon it the power to make them is accepted by those to whom they apply.

I conclude, therefore, that Hobbes is, in effect, drawing attention to an important feature of a legal system, provision for explicit legislation; but that this feature need not be possessed by all systems of rules. Indeed, the presence or absence of such a feature would be one way of distinguishing between a legal and a moral system. A professional code of conduct may but need not possess this feature, since it is not part of the idea of a profession that it either possesses or lacks it. It would be a mistake, therefore, to suppose that a profession which lacks a written code does not have a code of conduct at all; or, indeed, that it is necessarily an advantage to have a written code. Written codes, like written constitutions, possess both advantages and disadvantages, both of which should be taken into account.

iv
ENFORCEMENT

On the Hobbesian view, the possibility of formal legislation depends on the possibility of enforcement. I have tried to argue that this is not so. Nor is the reverse true; that is, that the possibility of enforcement depends on legislation, or even on explicit statement. It depends only on their *being* rules which, since they do not compel behaviour, may be broken; and further rules which specify the form which reaction to breaches of the primary rules must take. Nevertheless, if infringements of a code are to be punished, it is desirable that the code should be written down, so that those to whom it applies can know unambiguously and in advance whether or not their behaviour conforms to it. It is similarly desirable that the secondary judicial rules governing the practice whereby offences are established as offences and offenders punished should be explicitly stated in advance of particular cases.

To allow that a code of professional conduct may be enforced seems inconsistent with the view that professional persons are responsible in the sense that they do what they ought to do simply because they see that they ought to do it, since it seems to follow from that view that extraneous motivation in the form of penalties is unnecessary. In accepting collective responsibility for the conduct of its members, however, a profession is recognising the fact that it cannot assume that all its members will invariably act responsibly; and this is not inconsistent with the claim that in general its members are responsible. Willingness to take precautions against breakdowns in the system is evidence of collective responsibility rather than of individual irresponsibility. Acceptance of collective responsibility, indeed, is part of what is involved in the adoption of a code, since any code prescribes standards which are common to all those to whom it applies. The primary function of a professional code is to provide guidance to those to whom it applies; guidance provided by the profession collectively to its members individually. Moreover, as argued in the previous section, enforcement cannot replace individual responsibility entirely; it is at best a kind of safety net.

v

CRITICISM AND CHANGE

I have argued that rules and, therefore, systems of rules also depend for their existence on the behaviour of individuals. But whereas individuals, being subject to the laws of biology, have relatively fixed life-spans, systems of rules may persist indefinitely, since by their nature they incorporate mechanisms for their own perpetuation. To talk of a system of rules is simply a convenient way of talking about the settled manner in which the activities to which they relate are carried on by the individuals whose behaviour they regulate. Although brought into and kept in being through the actions and interactions of individuals, therefore, a system of rules has an existence which is independent of, and an identity which is separate from, that of any one individual or set of individuals. It provides a stable social framework which gives a sense and intelligibility to the behaviour of individuals which it would otherwise lack. The relation between the behaviour of individuals and the social framework in which they are located is reciprocal. On the one hand, the framework is constructed out of the behaviour of individuals; it makes no sense to suppose it could exist apart from that behaviour. On the other, the behaviour of those individuals could not be what it is if it were not located within that framework.

From this point of view, a system of rules may also be described as a social tradition. One way in which social traditions differ is in the extent to which they include provision for their own criticism. On the one hand, existing rules may be accepted uncritically on the authority of the previous generation. The type of society which results is said to be traditional, although 'tradition' is then being used to distinguish one *kind* of tradition from another. On the other hand, existing rules may be subject to constant criticism and revision on the basis of that criticism.

Social criticism is a relatively sophisticated exercise, requiring at least partial insight into the nature of social reality. It presupposes an awareness of rules as rules; that is, as entities which depend for their existence on the behaviour of the individuals to whom they apply and, therefore, which can be changed or modified by the collective action of those individuals. It is the realisation of this dependence, rather than the dependence itself, which makes criticism and suggestions for change possible. Secondly, criticism presupposes some awareness of the content of the rules being criticised; it may, indeed, begin with an explicit statement of them. Thirdly, criticism lacks point unless some view is taken of the purpose which the rules serve. Whereas for the traditionalist the existence of a rule is sufficient ground for its continued existence, the rational critic asks what human purpose it serves, whether it serves it efficiently and whether any alternative would serve it better.

It follows from the analysis in section 1 that all systems of rules which really exist and are not simply empty formulations do embody purposes, since the normal rule-abiding person has a reason, simply in being a member of the social group to which the rule applies, for behaving in the way required by it. The traditionalist's allegience to existing rules, therefore, is not devoid of purpose; it is just that he is unwilling to reflect on the purposes which he has acquired from his fathers. The social critic also, however radical his point of view may seem, cannot detach himself from the social tradition to which he belongs. Human purposes cannot be reduced to a common denominator, the nature of which can then be used to assess existing systems of rules. The difference between the traditionalist and the social critic, therefore, is not so much a difference between individuals but between those social traditions which include provision for their own criticism and those which do not.

vi
PROFESSIONAL CODES OF CONDUCT

I have tried to draw attention to dimensions along which systems of rules might differ, under the headings of scope and content, authoritative statement, formal legislation, enforcement and criticism and change. Legal and moral codes tend to occupy opposite ends of a spectrum on all these counts except the first. Both apply universally and may have the same content; laws, however, are the product of legislation and, therefore, are also stated both explicitly and authoritatively; they are usually enforced; and there is provision for criticism and change through the legislative procedures which produced them.

A code of professional conduct may approximate to a system of legal rules in these respects; or it may be more like a system of moral rules in lacking them. The advantage traditionally claimed for the rule of law is that it allows the individual to live his own life within the limits clearly set by the law; indeed, even the method of enforcement is primarily indirect, through the threat of punishment for law-breakers. A legal system, also, gains stability from its provision for enforcement and flexibility through its provision for legislation. A moral code, on the other hand, is less precisely defined and places greater reliance on the individual's sense of personal responsibility.

There is no obvious reason why a profession should adopt one model rather than the other. When demands for a professional code become vocal, however, it is the legal model which seems intended. They may be the result of the realisation that standards of personal responsibility are inadequate; or of the feeling that, in increasingly difficult and complex situations, the individual needs more external guidance; or, of course, on a variety of other factors. My purpose in this section, however, has not been to speculate as to the facts or to make highly general recommendations unrelated to the facts of particular cases but to draw attention to the options.

3
THE CONTENT OF A PROFESSIONAL CODE

In (i) of the previous section I suggested that codes of

professional conduct apply only to the members of the relevant profession when acting in their professional capacity; and that the sphere of activity of a profession is limited by its connection with specialised knowledge and skills. And I concluded that a code of professional conduct might be expected to concern itself with the proper use of that knowledge and skill in order to achieve most effectively the professional purposes which the members of the profession share. In this section, therefore, I will consider in more detail what content a code of professional conduct might be expected to have, paying particular attention to the teaching profession.

In chapter two I said that the most important aspect of a profession is the professional purpose which its members share; and drew attention to the independence — or freedom in determining and carrying out those purposes — which recognition as a profession brings. It is the profession which is granted a degree of autonomy in this way, not its members individually; and the profession which sets the standards to which its members must conform. According to the argument of the present chapter, however, a profession is neither more nor less than a living tradition as to how things should be done in the relevant field of practice; a social tradition is simply a relatively stable system of rules, that is, one having a recognisable historical dimension; and a system of rules, in turn, is no more than an abstract way of talking about the behaviour of individuals, including their behaviour towards one another. In the final analysis, therefore, a code of professional conduct will contain more or less what the members of the profession — past as well as present — want it to contain; it will set out their own wishes for their own professional practice. And what they will want will be to benefit personally from their professional activities and to achieve their professional purposes. I will deal with these in turn.

i

SELF-INTEREST

A code of professional conduct is likely to contain provisions which relate both to standards of payment and to the maintenance of public trust in and respect for the profession.

(a) *Payment.* In Western society the desire for material

prosperity is widespread and deep-rooted and extends, to a greater or lesser extent, to the professions. Accordingly, professional bodies, acting in a trade-union capacity, impose restrictions on entry to the profession and try to protect their members' incomes through salary negotiations or by imposing scales of minimum charges.

(b) *Public trust and respect.* In general people want very much to be trusted and respected by their fellow men, particularly in and for their performance in the job by which they earn their living. They also value, in their work, the freedom from supervision and, in their social lives, the status which public trust and respect, respectively, bring. Enjoying public trust and respect, also, they are more likely to be well paid. It is obviously in the personal interests of the members of a profession, therefore, that public trust in and respect for their profession be maintained; and codes of professional conduct typically contain provisions aimed at securing this end.

A miscellany of provisions come under this heading. Some have merely symbolic significance and relate, for example, to matters of dress. Stockbrokers, for example, wear morning dress when on the floor of the stock exchange, barristers wear white cravats when in court, and so on. Academic gowns are no longer worn universally; but most teachers feel the need to present a personal appearance consistent with their idea of the dignity of their profession. Others are related more directly to the performance of the relevant professional function, prescribing certain conduct as unprofessional or unethical. Solicitors, for example, must not speculate with clients' funds; police officers must not use undue pressure in interrogating suspects; teachers must not punish children with undue severity and so on. Such conduct may in any case be prescribed by law; but, whether it is or not, it is likely to be a matter of concern to the profession. Whatever brings a profession into disrepute damages the interests of its members as well as those of the community it serves.

ii

PROFESSIONAL PURPOSES

(a) *Questions of ends.* The most important part of a code of professional conduct will be concerned with the nature of the profession's purpose. Explicit statements of the overall purpose of a profession, such as teaching or the law, are difficult to make; and if made must be made in highly abstract terms and tend to be highly contentious. They are, therefore, unlikely to be included in an authoritative written code even if the profession happens to have one. Nevertheless, they are part of a code of conduct as defined in section 1, that is, as a system of written or unwritten rules. Rules have a point, or purpose, implicit in them; and a group of rules have an overall point in forming a unified system.

I have already given a general account of professional purpose in chapter two. In discussing the nature of a profession there, I said that a member of a profession acts as a principal acting in his own right rather than merely as an agent-for-another; the purposes which he strives to achieve are his own rather than set for him by anyone else. On the other hand, they are acquired from and shared with other members of the same profession. I argued also (in chapter two, section 4), first, that professional purposes relate to the interests of others and, secondly, that they relate to some special aspect of those interests. A member of a profession, therefore, is concerned to perform services for the rest of the community which he thinks are of value to it and which can be provided only by someone possessing the knowledge and skill which he possesses.

The identity of a profession, then, depends on the sense of purpose which its members share and are aware of sharing. Obviously the actual purpose which distinguishes one profession from another will depend on the profession concerned. The purpose of the medical profession, for example, is to promote health; that of the legal profession, to see that people receive justice; that of the Church, to bring people into close relation with God; that of the armed services, to protect their country, and so on. The purpose of the teaching profession is to educate; and in the next section I will draw attention to some of the problems connected with the question 'What is education?' Professional purposes, however, tend to be taken for granted within the profession itself, no attempt being made at explicit formulation. For the most part this does not matter, since over a wide range of circumstances the course of action dictated by them is clear and unambiguous.

(b) *Professional ethics*. Although I have defined a code of professional conduct broadly, most people tend to think of it more narrowly as an ethic peculiar to an individual profession.

A professional ethic has two functions: first, that of warning its members of the consequence to them of certain kinds of conduct and, secondly, that of guiding them in circumstances of special difficulty. In discussing public trust and respect I pointed out that the professions commonly condemn certain conduct as unprofessional or unethical. In doing so, however, the profession need not be acting solely, or even primarily, out of self-interest. Conduct which brings the profession into disrepute is also inconsistent with its overall purpose. Public trust and respect are themselves essential for efficient performance; and in most cases the inconsistency is also direct and obvious. For example, the interests of justice cannot be served if the police secure convictions by planting evidence or securing confessions under duress. Examples of this kind could easily be multiplied; they are possible in relation to any profession. In prescribing such conduct the profession is not informing its members of anything which they did not already know; it is simply warning them of the official disapproval or other penalty facing those caught acting in the forbidden way.

The second function of a professional ethic is more interesting. Circumstances may arise in which the individual practitioner, whilst wishing to remain true to his profession, is in genuine doubt as to what to do; and, therefore, feels the need for external guidance. The need is likely to be greatest in times of rapid social and technological change. The purpose of the medical profession, for example, is for the most part clear and uncontentious: it is to preserve life and to minimise suffering. Changing moral standards and technical progress, and the interaction between them, however, have combined to make these apparently clear aims difficult to interpret. Distinctions between life and death, health and sickness, treatment and research, and mental illness and crime which once seemed clear are no longer easy to make. The overall purpose of the medical profession remains more or less the same; and over a wide range of circumstances the course of action dictated by it is clear and unambiguous. Often, however, the individual practitioner is likely to welcome detailed practical advice about what to do in specified circumstances; for example, about whether to withdraw life-support systems once the brain has been irrevocably damaged; whether to give contraceptive advice to girls under the age of consent; whether to perform an abortion if the child, if born, will be mentally or physically handicapped; and so on.

Similar problems arise in other professions, although nowhere as clearly as in medicine. In teaching, for example, there is concern about the possibility that the teacher may make improper use of his influence over the minds of his pupils, indoctrinating rather than teaching or educating them. It is, however, extremely unclear what indoctrination is, despite extensive discussion of the concept of indoctrination in the recent literature of philosophy of education. The word 'indoctrination' seems to be used as a label for a miscellaneous group of teaching practices to which the speaker objects. What is objected to cannot be read off from the meaning of a word which is used as loosely as 'indoctrination'; but it does seem to be related to changing views about the purpose of education in a fast-changing political and social world. What is required is an explicit description of the practices which are held to be objectionable, which can then be discussed on their merits, rather than a definition of a word which is bound to be largely stipulative.

(c) *Questions of means.* In order to achieve its purposes a profession must not only have a clear idea as to what those purposes are, but also know how they can be achieved. Part of a code of professional conduct, therefore, will be concerned with questions of efficiency in achieving its purposes, that is, with questions of means. The knowledge and skill which allow a member of a profession to practise effectively would not normally be thought of as part of the profession's code of conduct. But the professional code is likely to stipulate minimum levels of competence, first, by insisting that only those who have passed an approved examination be allowed to practise and, secondly, by condemning as professionally incompetent those who appear to have forgotten or to have come to disregard what they originally learnt. In both cases the standards concerned are standards of efficiency. To the extent that they are well founded, anyone who ignores or disregards them is not only likely to be unsuccessful in his practice but also to be criticised or even debarred from practice by his colleagues. Taken together, the purpose of the practice and the rules of efficient practice provide criteria for what counts as, for example, a good teacher or doctor or, in other words, for what it is to be good at the practice of the relevant profession. A good doctor, for example, is one who is good at diagnosis, skilful in treatment and so on, and, therefore, one who may be expected, within the limits of available medical knowledge, to promote the health and well-being of his patients. A bad teacher or doctor, on the other hand, is one who either does not genuinely share the purpose of the profession and, therefore, who does not pursue it wholeheartedly; or who lacks the knowledge and skill needed to do so.

Questions of means and questions of ends cannot be wholly separated, since nothing counts as a means unless some end to the achievement of which it is taken to be the means is stated or taken for granted. To act rationally, in one sense of rational, is to choose ends which, in the light of past experience, may be expected to lead to the desired end. Means can be justified only by showing that they do lead to the desired end. Unless suitably qualified, therefore, the claim that the ends never justify the means is the reverse of the truth. What is true is that, in choosing means, all the consequences of their employment which relate to human purposes, including those not directly in question on the particular occasion, must be borne in mind if the behaviour is to count as fully rational. For example, the practice of pouring industrial waste into a river is justified, *prima facie*, by pointing out that it gets rid of the industrial waste; but this justification may be called into question by drawing attention to the effects on the environment of this method of waste disposal. The conflict which results, however, is not between ends and means as such, but between competing ends; that is, between the desire to dispose of waste products economically and the desire to preserve the natural environment from pollution.

In view of the dependence of means on ends, any ambiguity or disagreement about the purpose of a profession will be reflected in corresponding uncertainty or dispute about method. The purpose of the medical profession, for example, is relatively clear, despite the difficulties to which attention was drawn earlier: it is to preserve life and to minimise suffering. Consequently medical textbooks are able to state authoritatively how medical practice should be carried on. By contrast there is little agreement or clarity about the purpose of teaching, beyond the fact that it is education. As a result, books on teaching method seek to persuade and convert rather than to instruct impartially and authoritatively.

4
'WHAT IS EDUCATION?'

I have argued that a profession owes its existence to and is primarily identified by the purpose which its members share and are aware of sharing. Their day-to-day professional activities are directed towards a variety of proximate goals; but are co-ordinated by a sense of purpose which gives them an overall unity which would otherwise be lacking. And what distinguishes one profession from another is the particular purpose towards which its activities are directed and the nature of the expertise required for its achievement.

Teaching is distinguished from other professions by its concern for education; and this gives rise to the question 'What is education?' It is in any case obvious that this is a question of central importance for the philosophy of education. It has been avoided in the present enquiry, however, until the appropriate stage has been reached. The strategy adopted has been that of starting with the activities of teachers – that is, at what might be called the phenomenological level – and raising the relatively abstract question of the nature of education only after the correct context for it has been established.

Given that context, it is possible to see that the question is ambiguous as between a particular question or questions, which in turn have either a descriptive or prescriptive form, and a more general philosophical question. Each will be considered in turn;

all, however, are concerned in different ways with the nature of the overall purpose of the teaching profession.

i
THE PARTICULAR QUESTIONS

Questions are particular when asked about particular things. The question 'What is education?', therefore, is particular when asked in the context of and directed towards a particular educational tradition.

(a) *The descriptive question.* Teachers who keep an educational tradition alive through their professional activities may reflect upon and try to see more clearly the nature of their own activities; and their interest may, of course, be shared by others. In that context 'What is education?' is a question about the nature of the overall purpose of a particular group of people. It is taken for granted that their activities are educational and the question is concerned only with the particular form which they take. It is not an abstract question about the meaning of a word but an empirical question about the activities of a particular group of people. It can be answered, therefore, only by reference to the activities of those people.

It is not, however, easy to do briefly or directly. Perhaps the best way of doing so is by providing a description of the educational tradition concerned and its development. This, indeed, is what colleges of education normally provide for teachers undergoing initial training. For a full understanding of the English educational tradition, for example, it is necessary to know something about the rise of the grammar and public schools, the role of the Church in the development of elementary education, the introduction of the secondary and comprehensive schools, and so on. Such an account would inevitably contain a great deal of purely historical material, such as dates of legislation, methods of finance and inspection, numbers and ages of children in full-time education, and so on; and changes in education would have to be related to more general social and economic change. It would also, however, need to be a history of ideas which included an account of what the people responsible for important educational changes were trying to do; that is, an account of the purposes which motivated them. When such an account is brought up to date there is nothing further to learn about what education is in that educational tradition.

It is obvious, of course, that by no means all educational traditions are characterised by the presence of a teaching profession. There is no reason why teachers should not be what was referred to in section 3(iv) of chapter two as agents-for-another, obeying the orders of school boards, parents or politicians only in order to earn their living. Indeed, there may be educational traditions in which the role of teacher is totally absent, no one individual or group of individuals accepting any special responsibility for the education of the young. Whether we would still wish to call traditions so radically different from our own *educational* traditions can be decided only when an answer to the philosophical version of the question 'What is education?' is available.

(b) *The prescriptive question.* The question 'What is education?' may also be asked by those who are already familiar with the history and present position of the tradition within which it is raised. Their question is not what form that tradition takes, has taken or, indeed, will take but what form it ought to take in the future. It is still particular in being raised in the context of and about a particular educational tradition; but it is a different kind of question to that considered above. Questions about what changes should or ought to be made are logically distinct from questions about matters of empirical fact. To be relevant, answers to them must be based on the facts of the present situation and the possibilities of change which it contains; and these can be established only by consulting the relevant facts. But, within the limits imposed by those facts, they involve an irreducible element of choice or decision and, in that sense, are prescriptive. They lay down or prescribe what form the future is to take in so far as it is, or is thought to be, within human control.

Any educational tradition which makes provision for criticism and change is bound to be constantly seeking a better understanding of its own past and ways of improving upon it. In view of the logical dependence of questions of method on questions of ends, any suggestions for change are bound also to involve views about the purpose to be served by the proposed change, even if only implicitly. A radical view about the overall purpose of educational activity, indeed, may be presented in the form of detailed proposals for organisational changes; for example, from secondary modern and grammar to comprehensive schools or from universities to polytechnics. It may even be expressed in the form of actual institutions, such as particular schools, which provide a model which is later followed by others. This may, indeed, be the best way of expressing a new view of what education is all about. Attempts to do so explicitly may add little but high-minded phrases and tell us less than, for example, the knowledge that public schools are to be exempted from the proposed unification of secondary education. What is needed if we are really to know what people have in mind, in other words, is more detail, not less; just as the best way of answering the descriptive question considered above was by providing a detailed description of the present educational tradition and its development.

ii
THE PHILOSOPHICAL QUESTION

In either of the particular senses distinguished above, the question 'What is education?' must be related to a particular educational tradition before it can be answered. There is no possibility of answering it *a priori*, in abstraction from particular contexts. As pointed out earlier (in section 5(i)(a) of chapter three), there have been many groups of professional teachers, practising at different times and in different places; and there is no reason to expect all of them to have had exactly the same conception of what they were doing. Nevertheless, we should not recognise them as instances of the same profession unless their purposes were, in very general terms, the same. Accordingly, the question 'What is education?' may be a request for the principle of identity according to which we recognise different educational traditions as instances of the same kind of thing. It is when understood in this way that the question becomes philosophical.

It is important, at this stage, to make every effort to be quite clear what question is being asked and by whom it is being asked. The pronoun 'we' at the end of the previous paragraph refers to those who employ the principle of identity concerned; that is, those who possess a concept of education which they are able to apply to any tradition which they recognise as educational, including those of other societies as well as that of their own. An educational tradition, however, is a social phenomenon; this follows from the account of a social tradition given earlier in (v) of section 2. It is important, therefore, to recall the account of the nature of social phenomena in section 2 of the previous chapter. It was argued there that social phenomena characteristically possess a dimension, that of meaning, which physical phenomena lack; that they must be understood rather than simply observed; and they cannot be understood unless the concepts involved in them are grasped. The application to social phenomena of concepts which are alien to them, therefore, is a mistake which leads to their misidentification. Provided, however, social phenomena are first identified and described at what was called (in section 3 of the previous chapter) the ground-floor or phenomenological level, it is possible to apply to them higher-level concepts which are not necessarily available to those directly involved in them. The concept of education with which we are now concerned is a higher-level concept of this sort.

We possess a wide variety of higher-order concepts of this kind. Some incorporate cultural prejudice, beg the questions which they purport to raise or are pejorative or objectionable in other ways; for example, concepts like that of pre-logical thought, magic, savage and primitive. Others, however, are so familiar and uncontentious that their use easily goes unnoticed; for example, the group which centres on commercial transactions and the use of money. It seems beyond dispute that we are able to recognise transactions in a wide range of societies other than our own as commercial and to identify objects used in them as money. If this were not so we could not also talk about laws of economics which hold, inexorably, in all societies. The example of commerce will be considered further, therefore, before returning to education, the position of which is less clear.

There may be societies the members of which rely for their subsistence on food, such as fruit, berries and grubs, which requires only to be collected and eaten. Most, however, rely on more elaborate arrangements and make use of the division of labour. Provision must then be made for the distribution of the goods produced by the various specialist groups. This is usually done by a system of exchange, such as barter, although it could be done bureaucratically. Such a system is greatly improved by the introduction of money, which provides a recognised common denominator between the various goods to be exchanged and allows them to be distributed more efficiently. The value of money lies not so much in itself as in the goods for which it can be exchanged; but some system of accounting – whether in ledgers or through the use of money having physical existence and a characteristic physical appearance – must be used.

The story outlined in the previous paragraph is as old as Plato's *Republic*. It could be illustrated by a wide variety of examples, including that of primitive and isolated as well as advanced societies. The story itself, however, is general; and it is able to be general because the concepts which it uses – including property, economic exchange, distribution and money – need not be available to those to whom they are applied. That this is so is not immediately obvious. We are tempted to say that the members of an isolated South Sea island who use a special kind of shell as money, for example, must possess the concept of money. Their commercial behaviour, in being meaningful, involves the concept of the shell money which they use; and since shell money is money it seems as though they must possess the concept of money. Provided that, in saying that they possess the concept of money, we mean only that they possess the concept of shell money, this is correct. And it could be all that we did mean, since the word 'money' is often used as a synonym for the local form of money. There is, however, a logical difference between the higher-level concept of money and that of a particular form of it such as shell money which can be brought out by drawing attention to some of its consequences. The user of shell money need not realise, and might find it difficult to understand, that money could take any other form, such as metal coins or, more mysterious still, entries in bank ledgers. On the other hand, shell money may have religious or magical as well as commercial significance, in which case, although it is money, it is not simply money. More generally, we cannot spend money as such, any more than we can speak language as such; we can spend only particular forms of it, just as we can speak only particular languages. Indeed, the comparison with language is appropriate, since the concept of language is a similar higher-level concept which is applied cross-culturally without hesitation or thought.

Returning to education, the *kind* of question being considered should now be clear. It is a question about the concept of education which we employ when we speak of education as a kind of social phenomenon of which there is, or may be, more than one instance. Although that concept is *applied* cross-culturally, it is itself a concept which belongs to our own Western culture. It is our concept; it is to be expected, therefore, that it will reflect our own preoccupations and will be based on the paradigm provided by our own educational practice. Whether any other instances fall under it is, by contrast, an open question. In this respect it can be compared with our concept of law. We speak of English law, Roman law, American law and so on; but are doubtful whether so-called primitive law is really law. Nevertheless, our concept of education is not tied logically to our own educational tradition, any more than our concept of law is tied logically to our own legal tradition. It follows that a reference to, say, the English public school system (or to the curriculum enshrined in that system) is not part of what is meant by education, any more than a reference to the English jury system is part of what is meant by law.

The question, then, is how we identify a tradition as educational, whether our own or that of another society. Understood in this way, the question 'What is education?' is a question about the kind of overall purpose which has motivated different groups of people at different times and in different societies. In order to attain the required generality, any answer to it must be expressed in higher-level concepts which, like the concept of education itself, are not necessarily available to those directly involved. On the other hand, since our higher-level concept of education is bound to be based on the paradigm provided by our own educational tradition, any account of it will also be an account of our view of the purpose of education expressed in the most general terms possible.

My own view is that a social tradition is educational if its overall purpose is that others should become educated; and that to become educated is to learn to be a person. This preserves the connection between teaching as a profession and education referred to in section 2 of chapter one. In general, to teach is to help someone, perhaps on an isolated occasion, to learn something; but nothing is stipulated as to what must be learned. Professional teachers, however, accept responsibility for the learning of others and systematically set about trying to promote it; and the learning which they try to being about in them is that which leads to their becoming educated. What counts as becoming educated is laid down in detail by the particular educational tradition concerned; in general, however, to become educated is to learn to be a person.

I have elaborated and defended the view that to become educated is to learn to be a person elsewhere and will not go over the same ground now. There are, however, some points which it is appropriate to make in the present context. As pointed out above, the concepts in terms of which a higher-level concept like education is defined must themselves be higher-level concepts which can be applied cross-culturally; and the concepts of learning and that of a person both meet this requirement. I will consider them briefly from this point of view.

Learning is a second-order ability; that is, it is the ability to acquire other first-order abilities as circumstances require. Many animals other than man possess this ability; but the kinds of things which they can learn – that is, the range of abilities which they can acquire – is relatively limited. Human learning, on the other hand, is characteristically open-ended. What men learn depends not so much on innate dispositions which display themselves during a single lifetime as on the circumstances, especially the social circumstances, in which they find themselves. To put it another way, what they learn depends on the particular society into which they are born. Above all, they learn the ways of looking at things and behaving which are characteristic of that society; and in the course of doing so acquire also the shared concepts which make those ways of seeing things and behaving possible.

A person may be defined as the possessor of a scheme of such concepts. Earlier, it was argued that to speak of a social group or society is no more than a convenient way of talking about the persons who are its members and of the ways of looking at things and behaving which they share. One way of conceptualising their ways of behaving, which was considered at some length in section 1, is by talking about social rules and systems of social rules. To talk about a system of rules, it was argued, is simply a convenient but to some extent fictitious way of talking about the behaviour of the social group to whom the rules apply. The normal, rule-abiding person, in following a rule, is simply acting in accordance with a settled disposition which, since it is not innate, must have been acquired by a process of learning.

If we are prepared to talk of societies other than our own, therefore, we must also recognise their members as persons like ourselves and admit that they become persons through a process of learning. If we are to do this, however, the concepts of learning and of a person which we employ must be higher-level concepts. But we will also have to insist that, although the members of other societies are persons like ourselves, the kind of person they are will depend on the social traditions of the society to which they belong and to which they were introduced by a process of learning.

Finally, although it is true that the members of any society have to learn to become persons, it does not follow that there will be a group of people, in every society, whose job it is to help them to do so. In a simple society unplanned face-to-face contacts may suffice. Explicit, formal educational provision, with teachers accepting responsibility for the education of others, is a feature only of relatively large, complex societies like our own.

iii

THE POSSIBILITY OF A PRESCRIPTIVE ANSWER TO THE PHILOSOPHICAL QUESTION

Earlier in this section I distinguished between a descriptive and a prescriptive answer to the question 'What is education?' when raised in the context of a particular educational tradition.

No similar distinction was made, however, when the question was interpreted as a request for the principle of identity according to which different educational traditions are recognised as educational. It was taken for granted that the answer which was given to it – that a tradition is educational when its purpose is to help others to become persons – was descriptive. I want to consider now whether it could be taken prescriptively.

It is not easy to see how such a statement could be interpreted prescriptively. There is no question of persons becoming persons other than by a process of learning, for example, of their being manufactured or born as complete, fully functioning adults. It could be argued that this is a contingent matter; but even if the argument were admitted, it is still beyond dispute that it is the case. It is doubtful, also, whether much sense could be made of a suggestion that human societies should be made up of some kind of entity other than persons; for example, of social insects which are creatures of instinct. In changing the terms of the relational web which makes up a society the nature of the whole would be changed also. It is doubtful, therefore, whether any alternative to education could be intelligibly conceived; and in the absence of alternatives there is no scope for prescription.

It is possible for one society to attempt to impose its own idea of what a person should be on another. Something of this sort may have happened when the missionary societies set up schools in various parts of the world. Similarly, the modern assertion of a universal right to education may amount in practice to the claim that everyone should have a Western-style education. But a society which tries to carry out such a policy is, in effect, trying to assimilate the other society into its own; and the prescription on which it acts is particular.

It was pointed out earlier that, although it is necessarily true that all societies are made up of persons and that all persons have to learn to become persons, some societies make no formal provision for education. And the assertion of a universal right to education could be interpreted as the claim that all of them ought to do so. It is difficult, however, to see how alien institutions could be introduced into a society without changing its character, and, therefore, that of its members. A policy of this sort, therefore, would be indistinguishable from that considered in the previous paragraph.

The difficulty of taking the answer to the question 'What is education?' prescriptively is due partly to the way in which it has been answered; that is, to the definition of 'becoming educated' as 'learning to be a person'. The concept of a person is basic to our understanding of social phenomena, just as the concept of a physical object is basic to our understanding of physical phenomena; and the concept of learning is linked to that of a person almost as closely as the concept of a cause is linked to that of a physical object. There is no room, therefore, for a prescriptive interpretation of education as so defined. If an alternative definition were offered which kept much closer to the paradigm provided by our own educational tradition, the prospect of its being interpreted prescriptively would be greatly improved. In other words, we might say that we are not prepared to recognise any tradition as educational unless it conformed, in greater or less detail, to our own. But, in being prescriptive, the definition could no longer function as a principle of identity; it could not be used to recognise different educational traditions as instances of the same kind of thing. It would, therefore, cease to be philosophical. Moreover, it could not even function prescriptively outside the tradition of its origin unless some other cross-cultural concept of education were covertly adopted.

5
THEORY OF EDUCATION

I have little to add under the heading of theory of education to what has been said already, especially in chapter two, section 2, about the specialised knowledge and skill required for efficient professional practice and in section 3 of the present chapter about the content of a professional code. It follows from what has been said there that if, as Professor D. J. O'Connor claims in *An Introduction to the Philosophy of Education*, the word 'theory' as used in educational contexts is no more than a courtesy title, then the courtesy is misplaced, since what is called educational theory is in fact an integral part of educational practice. And what I have been trying to do throughout this book is to give an account of educational practice in which the need for special knowledge and skill is fully recognised.

The knowledge concerned, for example about the conditions favourable to learning, is itself theoretical, in the sense that statements of it are, or are taken to be, true and may form part of an elaborate theory of learning. When such statements are collected and organised in order to help teachers to practice more efficiently, however, the body of knowledge which results owes its unity to the purpose for which it was collected; and that purpose was practical. There is, moreover, no oddity in the suggestion that the making of theoretical statements − that is, statements which can be either true or false − is part of what is involved in taking part in a practical activity such as education. On the contrary, it would be odd to suggest that a practical activity could be carried on which did not involve beliefs, and expressions of belief, about the appropriateness of the methods adopted to achieve the ends of the activity. Indeed, such statements are likely to be prominent when the activity concerned forms part of an educational tradition which encourages criticism and change.

It would be pedantic to object to the use of the term 'educational theory' to refer to statements made in the course of educational practice which also have a place in and probably originated in a theoretical activity such as psychology or sociology. I will therefore permit myself a guarded use of it. In the exchange of views between Professors D. J. O'Connor and Paul Hirst in *New Essays in the Philosophy of Education*, however, neither interprets educational theory in such a restricted way. This can be shown by considering briefly some of the points which they are concerned to make.

Professor O'Connor points out that educational theory does not consist of a logically interconnected set of hypotheses and, therefore, fails to conform to the paradigm provided by a scientific theory. In a scientific theory, however, the logical connection between hypotheses is achieved by moving to a more abstract level through the introduction of theoretical concepts. The individual hypotheses to be unified by the theory are then deduced from highly abstract principles which make use of those concepts. The logically interconnected whole, consisting of abstract scientific principles and empirical hypotheses deduced from them, then constitutes the scientific theory. In the case of educational theory, however, the position is very different. Statements are included in it only because they are relevant to the practice of education, the principle of relevance for their inclusion being provided by the overall purpose of the particular educational practice concerned. Once admitted, they form part of that practice and automatically share its unity. Educational theory does not *fail* to be a theory in the scientific sense, therefore, as Professor O'Connor suggests, since it is the wrong sort of thing either to fail to be or to succeed in being such a theory.

Professor Hirst, on the other hand, recognises the practical nature of educational theory; but at the same time insists that it *is* theory and presumably, therefore, not part of educational practice. It is able to guide practice, however, because it includes value judgements. The making of value judgements, moreover, is taken to be the same kind of operation as the discovery of psychological truths – a difficult operation but one which, if carried out in the proper manner, is capable of yielding truths which are incontrovertible and universal. The educational theory which results is similarly universal and available to guide educational practice everywhere. It is not tied logically to the particular educational tradition for which it was designed but is just as relevant to any other educational tradition.

I do not think that there is such a thing as educational theory in this sense. The belief in the possibility of discovering values which are objective and universal, whether educational or otherwise, is mistaken. What has or lacks educational value is laid down within particular educational traditions by those taking part in them. To put it another way, Professor Hirst's view presupposes the possibility of a prescriptive answer to the philosophical question 'What is education?'; and this was discussed and rejected in the previous section. It is possible, as was pointed out there, to try to impose your own idea of education on others; but not to justify doing so on the grounds that that is what education really is.

Both Professor O'Connor and Professor Hirst see educational

theory as something separate from educational practice rather than as an integral part of it. This leads Professor O'Connor into thinking that an educational theory ought to possess the same sort of unity as a scientific theory; and Professor Hirst into thinking that the empirical part of educational theory can be related to educational practice only if it is first combined, in some unspecified and unspecifiable manner, with universal objective values. Both views are mistaken for basically the same reason – their failure to take the notion of a social practice sufficiently seriously.

CHAPTER FOUR: NOTES AND REFERENCES

1(i) It is tempting to say that rules are logical constructions out of the behaviour of individuals. The term 'logical construction', however, belongs to the vocabulary of reductive analysis and might be taken to carry with it the suggestion that rules (together with social groups, communities, etc) are, in Bentham's terms, merely fictitious entities which do not really exist. Bentham describes the community as 'a fictitious *body*, composed of the individual persons who are considered as constituting as it were its *members*' (*The Principles of Morals and Legislation*, p. 341 in British Moralist, vol. 1, edited by L. A. Selby-Bigge). And a fictitious entity is defined as 'an entity to which, though by the grammatical form of discourse employed in speaking about it, existence is ascribed, yet in truth and reality existence is not meant to be ascribed' (p. 10 in *Bentham's Theory of Fictions* edited by C. K. Ogden). In my view, however, rules, social groups and communities do exist. But they exist as social entities and, therefore, in the manner appropriate to social pheonomena. They depend for their reality on what they are taken to be and, therefore, on people and their behaviour. They are also dependent on people so far as their identification is concerned. Persons, who possess physical bodies, and their behaviour can be identified directly, when as rules, etc., which possess only social reality can be identified only indirectly. Professor P. F. Strawson draws attention in *Individuals* (pp. 40 ff) to the way in which the identification of a particular of one type, such as a sensation or mental event, is dependent on that of a particular of another type, such as a person.

The development of philosophical analysis and its connection with the metaphysics of atomism is described in detail in J. O. Urmson's *Philosophical Analysis*. It is the metaphysics of atomism rather than the method of analysis as such which I am rejecting in this book as inappropriate to an understanding of the nature of social phenomena.

The account of rules given in the text, according to which rules function primarily as guides to behaviour, is based on that of Professor H. L. A. Hart in *The Concept of Law*.

2(iii) The best known statement of Hobbes's views is contained in *Leviathan*. Hobbes's view of laws as commands backed by force, or threat of force, was followed by Bentham and, in turn, by Austin in *The Province of*

Jurisprudence Determined. Its criticism and rejection are the negative plank in Hart's *The Concept of Law.*

3(ii)(b) Indoctrination is discussed in *Concepts of Indoctrination,* a collection of papers edited by I. A. Snook. Snook puts forward his own views in *Indoctrination and Education.*

4(ii) I put forward the view that to become educated is to learn to be a person in chapter 5 of *Philosophy and Education* and in 'The concept of education' in *New Essays in the Philosophy of Education,* edited by Glenn Langford and D. J. O'Connor.

4(iii) In *The Logic of Education* Professors P. H. Hirst and R. S. Peters put forward an account of the concept of education which claims to be philosophical whilst also having 'important general implications for the curriculum, for teaching, for relationships with pupils and for the organisation of the educational community' (p. 15). They would, however, be reluctant to call their account prescriptive, since they hold the view that the implications concerned can be objectively justified in a strong sense of objective. Whether this is a tenable position depends on whether sense can be given to the notion of objective justification in the relevant sense. It follows from the view expressed in the text that in my view this cannot be done. (In this connection, see also my essay 'Values in Education' in *New Essays in the Philosophy of Education.*)

The social context of a profession

1
MEMBERSHIP OF A PROFESSION AND ITS CLIENTS

i

MEMBERS

In the preceding chapters I have tried to present a view of teachers as members of a teaching profession rather than as isolated individuals; but so far have failed to relate the teaching profession to *its* social context. It might be said, therefore, that so far I have been looking at education with the myopic gaze of a goldfish in a goldfish bowl.

In the following sections I will try to remedy this. Before doing so, however, I would like to consider two ways in which, it might be claimed, too narrow a view has been taken of the teaching profession itself. I have spoken, for the most part, as though membership were confined to those who actually teach in the classroom; that is, to what might be called classroom teachers. But, although classroom teachers do provide the core of the teaching profession, they could not do their job in a complex modern community without the organisation and services provided by others. In a large school, for example, the Head and, perhaps, his deputy may spend little or no time actually teaching in the classroom; but they co-ordinate the work of others to try to make sure that no aspect of the education of the children attending the school is neglected. Similarly the various educational institutions combine to form educational systems; there are, therefore, also local education officers, central government officials, inspectors of schools and specialist advisers of all kinds.

Whilst, therefore, there would not be a teaching profession unless its membership included classroom teachers, there is no reason why it should be confined to them. They provide a paradigm to which others conform to a greater or less extent; but there is no sharp line dividing members from non-members. In accordance with the argument of chapter three, questions about who is and who is not a member of which profession are questions of fact, to be decided by reference to the facts of each case in accordance with the criteria laid down in chapter two. The knowledge and skill criterion, in particular, provides the most obvious way of discriminating between the various groups of people who are connected, in one way or another, with educational institutions and the educational system without actually being classroom teachers. On the one hand, head teachers and school inspectors might be included and, on the other, school cooks, cleaners, janitors and so on, whose expertise lies elsewhere, excluded. But any lines drawn would be to some extent arbitrary and artificial. The teaching profession merges into the wider context of work and life, rather than being discrete and separate from it.

Other professions are equally ill defined in their denotation. In the case of medicine, for example, a sharp distinction is drawn between doctors and nurses; and there may be real differences between them in the extent of their knowledge and skill, and in the burden of responsibility which they carry. Most people, however, would consider nurses to be as much a part of the medical profession as doctors. But there are many other people whose position is less clear; for example, administrators, medical social workers, hospital porters, ambulance drivers and so on.

To conclude, then, the view taken of the membership of a profession may have seemed unduly narrow; but it was taken for convenience of exegesis only. It was not intended to beg any factual questions for or against any particular group of people.

ii

CLIENTS

Membership of the teaching profession, then, may not be confined to those who regularly engage in face-to-face contacts

with schoolchildren or students. There is, however, a second
respect in which the account given might be thought too narrow
in concentrating on teachers to the exclusion of the children or
students they teach. This could hardly be a criticism of the
account of the teaching profession, since it could not be argued
that schoolchildren or students, or what might be referred to
more generally as a profession's clients, are part of the
profession itself. It could be argued, however, and far more
radically, that it was a mistake to concentrate on teachers in the
first place rather than on those they teach.

I do not wish to deny, however, that the child or, more
generally, the client, has a point of view which should not be
neglected. But the relations which the members of a profession
have with their clients depend for their identity and character on
the former rather than the latter; and, therefore, can be
understood only by concentrating on the former. This does not
reflect any kind of value judgement to the effect that teachers are
more important than their pupils, doctors than their patients,
lawyers than their clients, and so on. Indeed, it was part of the
idea of a profession that professional purposes are characterised
by their concern for others. And, since the members of a
profession are motivated in this way, it follows that teachers
think children's education important, doctors think patients'
health important, and so on. To this extent at least, therefore, the
point of view of the child is not neglected.

But although it is essential to the idea of teaching as a
profession that the interests of the child should be consulted –
indeed, that they are the primary consideration – this leaves
open the question as to who shall decide where those interests
lie. A similar question arises in the case of other professions,
although no problem arises if profession and client are in
agreement; for example, when a sick patient wants to get well.
But there are bound to be disagreements in many cases. For
example, a defendant faced with a criminal charge will almost
certainly want to be acquitted even if he is guilty; whereas the
defence lawyer is concerned only to see that he is not found
guilty if he is innocent. As a member of a profession, a lawyer
shares the purpose of his profession, that of securing justice for
all rather than promoting the interests of some individuals at the

expense of those of others. In the case of teaching, the position is complicated by the fact that, in general, the profession's clients are children; and, children *being* children, it cannot be taken for granted, in this or any other context, that they are the best judges of their own interests. Young children have no considered or balanced view of their own interests, or indeed any conception of them beyond the whim of the moment. Part of what is involved in their becoming educated, however, is their acquisition of such a conception. As they grow older, therefore, they come to have a view of their own interests which can be consulted or ignored. Children also normally have parents who are concerned, to widely varying degrees, about their children's education.

Although, therefore, the teacher is concerned to promote the interests of the child, it does not follow that his is the only view of those interests. He must, however, come to some conclusion about the child's interests; otherwise he will not be in a position to act to promote them. In arriving at that conclusion there are reasons why he should take the view of the child and his parents into account; but there are also reasons why they cannot be accepted as the sole guide. On the one hand there are, first, arguments of the kind advanced in Mill's essay, *On Liberty*, which appeal to a principle of self-determination and, secondly, arguments of a pragmatic kind based on the improved chances of success if the co-operation of child and family is obtained. On the other hand, there are very good reasons why the teacher must rely to a large extent on his own judgement. First, the view of the child or parent is obviously partisan, whereas the teacher has to consider the interests of all those with whom he has to deal. Secondly, children and parents are often ignorant of the possibilities of the situation – both of the facilities which the school is able to offer and of the extent to which the individual child is able to benefit from them. And, thirdly, the teacher will often adopt a paternalistic view, preferring his own view of the child's interests to that of either the child or its parents.

I do not intend to argue here for or against paternalism, beyond pointing out that it is a point of view which one would expect most teachers to share to a large extent. It is a view which virtually every parent takes; it cannot be argued, therefore, that paternalism is somehow a wicked or immoral point of view. And to a limited extent the position of a teacher is similar to that of a parent. It would be wrong, therefore, to dismiss the paternalistic point of view simply on the grounds that it is the opposite of the liberal or self-deterministic view. The view which it is appropriate to take depends very much on the context; it is obviously objectionable, for example, to treat normal responsible adults as though they were children. I have tried, therefore, to locate the context, within teaching, in which this issue arises; and have refrained from arguing as though one view or the other was, on *a priori* grounds, exclusively correct.

There are many other interesting questions which might be raised about the relationship between a profession and its clients, some of which are considered in professional ethics; for example, questions of confidentiality and about conflicts of loyalty to client and to employer. It would, however, take me too far from my main theme, and perhaps into the realm of casuistry, to consider them further here.

2
THE IDEA OF A COMMUNITY

In the previous section I drew attention to two ways in which the account of a profession which has been given so far might be thought too narrow; but concluded that in neither case was this so. The account would be incomplete, however, unless some consideration were given to the social context of a profession. It has been taken for granted that the members of a profession form a social group only within and as part of a larger social group or community, not only in the account of a profession itself but also in the account of education in section 4 of the previous chapter and in the characterisation of sociology and anthropology in section 3 of chapter three. Some account of what a community is, therefore, will be given in this section; and the nature of the relationship between a profession and the community of which it forms a part will be considered in the following section.

i

THE IDEA OF A COMMUNITY

Since a community is a social phenomenon, I will begin by recalling the general account of the nature of social phenomena and social groups which was given in chapter three. It was argued there that social phenomena typically possess a dimension, that of meaning, which physical phenomena lack; and this was taken to mean that they involve the possession and use of concepts. They must, therefore, be understood rather than, simply, observed; and to understand them is to grasp the concepts involved in them. Unless this is done they will not be correctly identified as social phenomena at what was called the phenomenological level; but when it is done the observer necessarily comes to see what the person is doing as the person himself sees it. A more complex kind of social phenomenon arises when a number of people not only share ways of looking at things and behaving but are also aware of sharing them and, in what was called reciprocal self-awareness, are aware that they are aware of sharing them. The way in which reciprocal self-awareness alters a person's social situation in what was called a primary social group was explored in chapter four, in which the idea of a social rule which discriminates amongst the ways of behaving which would otherwise be open to a person was explored. Finally, allowance was made for the possibility of describing and classifying social phenomena in terms of concepts not involved in the phenomena themselves, provided they are first identified as social phenomena at the phenomenological level. The example used to illustrate this was that of the farmer described as contributing to the apple glut, even though, so far as he was aware, he was simply picking and marketing apples.

A community is obviously a social group of a kind. Indeed, 'community' and 'society' are virtual synonyms and it might be thought that there was nothing further to be added to the account given earlier and summarised above. This is not so, however, for two reasons. First, the idea of a community is that of a social group which, although itself containing other social groups, is not a member of any larger social group. In other words, it is the idea of a totality which has a kind of completeness and self-sufficiency which its parts lack, and which is comparable to the kind of completeness which the life of a person has as compared with one of its aspects or which an organism has as compared with one of its organs. And, secondly, although a community is a social group of a kind, it cannot be taken for granted that it is a primary social group of the kind considered in chapter three.

In (ii) below, therefore, I will consider the idea of completeness involved in the idea of a community and in (iii) the question of what kind of social group a community is.

ii

A COMMUNITY AS A COMPLETE EXISTENT

The completeness which a community has has been compared with that of a person or an organism; the sense in which each is a complete existent will therefore be considered.

(a) *A person as a complete existent.* Earlier persons have been thought of as having the ability to acquire and use concepts and, therefore, to make observations and behave and to enter into social relations with other persons in primary social groups. But, whilst persons *are* members of primary social groups, such as professions, their lives extend beyond their participation in the activities of any one such group and their interests beyond the achievement of its relatively limited purposes. A doctor, for example, is professionally concerned about the health of his patients; but he may also have a wife and family, enjoy good food and the company of his friends, like to go to the theatre and to play golf and so on. When we say that a person is a doctor, therefore, we are talking about one aspect of his life, not the whole of it. His work may be – indeed, it is likely to be – an important part of his life; but no one, however dedicated, can be *just* a doctor. The first point, then, is that the life of a person has a certain degree of complexity in being made up of aspects and, although we can speak of one of those aspects to the neglect of others, in doing so we are necessarily speaking of something which is a part of a larger whole.

Secondly, the things which a person does do not form an arbitrary collection, like the class of red-headed people who happen to live in the same town, but are united, together with his experiences, memories and emotions, in being the activities of one and the same person. The doctor in his surgery is the same person as the one who later plays golf, has tea with his family, watches television and goes to bed. Seeing his activities as united in this way is not only not arbitrary but, given that we have the concept of a person which we do have, unavoidable; for our concept of a person is that of a separate existent or being which, although complex in having parts or aspects, is complete in itself. It may be related to other things; but does not have to be so related in order to be the thing which it is.

The points made in the two preceding paragraphs – that the life of a person has many aspects which, taken together, constitute a complete existent – can be illustrated by an example used earlier, that of a farmer picking apples. Any description of him as an apple picker, although correct as far as it goes, would necessarily be incomplete, since it makes no sense to suppose that a person's sole purpose in life could be to pick apples, although it might be the sole purpose of a machine. Even as an apple farmer he would have to occupy himself in many other ways, such as pruning, spraying, cutting the grass in the orchard, packing and marketing fruit and so on; and, almost certainly, in such activities as calculating the pay and deductions of his workers, keeping accounts, claiming subsidies and so on. He might, also, be engaged in other farming activities which would involve him in ploughing, harrowing and sowing; there are also all the things which he would do as church warden, husband and father, and regular at the local, and other simple acts like pausing in his work to admire the elm trees outlined against the skyline. All these different things combine harmoniously to form the life of one person, John Brown. It is not easy to state the principle in accordance with which they are so combined. Each aspect of his life, however, may be thought of as, or as reflecting, a settled purpose which directs a part of his behaviour; and he himself as the sum of such purposes. John Brown is then complex in being made up of parts, such as Farmer Brown the apple picker, which combine to form the life of a complete person.

It might be objected that this view of what a person is is inadequate and that the idea of a person who need not be a member of any social group makes little sense. A person, therefore, is a complete existent only in a relative sense. This is in line with the argument of the previous pages; but it does not affect the analogy between a community and a person as conceived above, which was intended only to bring out the sense in which the idea of a community is that of a complete existent. The same point can be made, perhaps more clearly, by comparing a community with an organism.

(b) *An organism as a complete existent.* The word 'organism' is really no more than a synonym for 'living thing'. A community, however, is often compared not with a living thing as such but with its body. In other words, the animal's overt behaviour is ignored and attention paid only to the internal organisation of its body. This, like the concept of a person referred to above, is a simplification, since the body concerned must be that of a living thing; and the idea of a living thing which does not respond to its environment makes little sense. I will therefore take it that an organism is a complete living thing; but will concentrate attention on its body rather than on its behaviour.

An organic body is a complex whole which has a completeness and self-sufficiency which its parts, or organs, lack. It is true that there is a sense in which an eye, for example, may be complete or incomplete, depending on whether some part of it, such as the cornea, is missing. An eye, however, must always be an eye *of* something, for example of a cat; in identifying an isolated eye as an eye we would automatically be assuming that it had once formed a part of a complete animal. The idea of an eye, in other words, is the idea of a part of some more complex whole; whereas the idea of a cat is that of an independent existent. We insist on seeing things in this way not only because that is how things are presented to us by nature – we normally meet complete animals rather than their isolated organs – but also because we know from experience that whereas an animal is able to survive and, therefore, to preserve its identity over a period of time, an isolated organ is not. Barring accidents, an eye in an animal body tends to last for the lifetime of the animal; but, once separated from it, soon begins to decompose. There are, in other words, certain natural facts which make this way of looking at things inevitable.

A COMMUNITY AS A SOCIAL GROUP

The idea of a community has been compared with that of a person and of an organism in order to bring out the sense in which it is that of a complex whole which has a kind of completeness which its parts lack. The question to be considered now is that of the kind of principle which unites its parts into such a complete existent or totality.

(a) *The principle of unity of a person.* It was pointed out above that all the things which a person does combine harmoniously to form the life of one person; but no suggestion was made as to *how* they combine. It was simply asserted that as a matter of fact we do and, perhaps, cannot but see them in that way. We are able to do so because the same physical body is involved on each occasion: but of course the unity of a person's life is not the same as that of their body.

It is not easy to say what gives a person's life its unity. A partial answer, which may be sufficient for present purposes, is that it is provided by the unity of his outlook and purposes. A person is not just identified as a person by others but has some conception of himself as a purposive being which dictates, within the limits open to him, his choice of livelihood and manner of living and, more generally, gives structure and meaning to his life. The limited purposes which its various aspects reflect form a harmonious whole because they are part of a unified view of how to live. The thing to do at such and such a time and place, for example, is to pick apples; but with a realisation that, earlier in the year, the trees were sprayed and the blossom was protected from the frost and that, when picked, the apples will be packed and marketed. In short, the unity of a person's life is a unity of purpose.

If a community is thought of as like a person in this respect, therefore, the second question raised in (i) above, about the kind of social group a community is, can now be answered. A person is like a primary social group in that his existence, as a person, depends on his own conception of himself and of his purposes; and his purposes form an ordered hierarchy in which some are subordinate to others and all are reconciled by a sense of overall purpose. If a community is like a person in this respect, therefore, it is a kind of primary social group, distinguished from others by its completeness. And it depends for its unity on the fact that its members see themselves and each other as members and, therefore, as sharing a comprehensive way of looking at things and behaving.

(b) *The principle of unity of an organism.* It was pointed out in (ii)(b) above that the idea of a part of an organism, such as an eye, is the idea of a part of some more complex whole, such as a cat; whereas the idea of a cat is not. In other words, the identification of a part of an organism depends on a prior identification of the whole of which it is a part. So far as identification is concerned, therefore, we move, in general although not in each individual case, from the whole to the part.

This does not tell us how the parts of an organism are combined to form a complete unified organism. Anatomists and physiologists, however, have had considerable success in answering this question. The parts of an animal's body are related causally to each other and to the external environment in such a way as to form a stable, self-maintaining system within that environment. In other words, living, healthy animals have stable identities because their parts are causally related to each other in the way in which they are. And the parts of an animal's body are identified by their function; that is, by reference to the contribution which they make – and are able to make because of their causal properties – to the continued existence or survival of the organism as a living thing of its own kind.

The task of the physiologist, therefore, is complex. He has first to identify a living thing as a living thing of a particular kind, such as a cat; it is fundamental to the logic of biological enquiry that he must start at this point. He has then to see the cat as complex in being made up of parts or organs; and he has to understand the way in which those parts interact causally to form a stable system. What was initially identified as a single animal, a cat, comes to be seen as a complex but stable causal system.

If a community is thought of as like an organism in this respect, therefore, a community is not a primary social group at all but a social group of a different kind which I will call a casual social group. The parts of an organism do not perform their function in order to – that is, with the conscious purpose of – ensuring the survival of the organism of which they are a part. Unlike persons, they have no conception of themselves and of what they are doing. They simply possess chemical and physical properties and interact with each other as they do because they possess those properties and are spatially related to each other as they are in the living body to which they belong. By analogy, therefore, a community is a complex whole the parts of which interact causally with each other to form a stable system. To find out *what* the parts are it is necessary to find out what interacts causally with what and, in so doing, contributes to the stability of the whole community. But, if there are to be any grounds for regarding a community as a social phenomenon of any kind, the parts must be, or must include, social phenomena at the phenomenological level, for example, persons and primary social groups; but may also include causal social groups which lack the completeness of a community.

Two points must be made about a community as so conceived. The idea of such a community takes it for granted that causal relations can intelligibly be said to exist not only between physical bodies but also between the sorts of things which form the parts of a community. Whether this is so will depend on the view taken of the nature of causality and of social phenomena; but it does not seem to be excluded either by the Humean view of causality as constant conjunction or by the account of social phenomena given earlier. Purposive behaviour has both intended and unintended consequences; and there is no reason why those consequences should not be related to the behaviour in a lawful manner. It was pointed out earlier, for example, that although a man may see himself simply as picking apples, his behaviour may as a matter of fact have the unintended consequence of increasing the apple glut. More generally, the market price of a commodity is the result of the interaction of the behaviour of the many individuals who buy and sell in that market. Each behaves purposively, in accordance with his own personal preference, which is to sell as dearly or buy as cheaply as the market allows. The actions of sellers, however, tend to cause the price to fall and the actions of buyers to cause it to rise, although neither of these consequences was intended by the parties concerned. It is also possible, although less usual, for buyers to buy or sellers to sell in order to cause the price to rise or fall, for example when manipulating share prices in the stock market or rates of exchange in a currency market. They are able to do this because they understand the way the market works. Individual purposes, therefore, interact causally in accordance with what is called the market mechanism or the laws of supply and demand.

Secondly, whereas the physiologist must start his enquiry with the identification of whole animals, only then going on to discover how they are made up of parts, the sociologist must begin with the parts, or putative parts, of a community, identifying them in the first instance not *as* parts but in some other way, for example as persons, or primary or causal social groups; and only then trying to discover the causal relations which obtain between them. It follows, also, that whereas it is a presupposition of biological enquiry that the world contains living things, it must be an open question whether the world contains communities, that is causal social groups possessing the required completeness and self-sufficiency.

iv
THE COMPATIBILITY OF THE PURPOSIVE AND CAUSAL VIEWS OF A COMMUNITY

In (ii) I tried to elucidate, by means of comparisons with a person and an organism, the idea of a community as a complete existent; and in (iii) I raised the question as to whether a community is a kind of primary or a kind of causal social group. The comparison with a person suggests what I will call a purposive view of a community. On this view the idea of a community is that of a rational construction which reflects the purposes of its members, who are seen as sharing a vision of the good life and co-operating to achieve it. The comparison with an organism, on the other hand, suggests what I will call a causal view of a community. According to it, a community is simply the chance result of the interaction of causal forces; and the final form which it takes is independent of human purposes.

There is no obvious incoherence in either the purposive or causal view of a community. It is therefore primarily an empirical matter which is best suited to the phenomena or, indeed, whether anything corresponds to either conception. In order to consider the relationship between a profession and the community of which it forms part, however, some view must be adopted as to how the two views are related. At first sight it looks as though they are mutually exclusive; and to the extent that each is thought of as representing the whole truth this may be so. The unity of an anthill, for example, seems to rest solely on causal interaction between its members; whilst that of a community of angels may rest only on their unity of purpose. There is no *a priori* reason, however, why a community of persons should not rest on both causal interaction and purpose. Indeed, it is doubtful whether much sense could be made of the idea of ordinary human purposes unless a context in which causes produce their effects in a known and reliable way is assumed.

This becomes clear if the need for and possibility of social planning are considered. It is obvious that communities may possess features which their members would wish to change if they thought it were possible for them to do so. Large-scale unemployment, poverty, disease, ignorance and crime could hardly be valued for their own sake, even if they are regarded as unavoidable or are accepted as necessary for the achievement of other social ends. Their presence in a community cannot, therefore, reflect any settled purpose on the part of its members. Nor is this conclusion surprising. The purposive view rested on an analogy between a community and a person; and for the purpose of that analogy, a person was presented as a complete existent, the unity of which was a unity of purpose. In fact, however, people are neither as rational nor as fully in control of themselves and their circumstances as this suggests; the form which their lives take owes as much to accident and external circumstance as to any settled purpose of their own. It is not to be expected, therefore, that a community which consists only of persons and the relations between them would reflect, without ambiguity or distortion, the purposes of its members.

The causal view is similarly one-sided. If it represented the whole truth, it would follow that any attempt at social planning was misconceived, since the form which a community took would depend only on impersonal forces and could not be modified in accordance with the wishes of its members. In fact, however, we believe that social planning is possible, even although we also have reason to believe that it is difficult. One can imagine a community the members of which had no conception of social planning; but even in such a community we believe that it would be possible if its members came to acquire such a conception.

Social planning, therefore − the attempt to realise social purposes − is, on the one hand, pointless if such purposes are already fully realised and, on the other, impossible if the form which a community takes depends only on impersonal causal forces. It is, however, neither pointless nor impossible. Putting the matter positively, social planning involves the adoption of some end to be realised through planning (and, therefore, presupposes some purpose not already realised); and of some method of achieving that end (and, therefore, presupposes some knowledge of methods which can be expected to be effective.) For example, government action designed to avoid large-scale unemployment both involves the adoption of avoidance of unemployment as an end and presupposes some knowledge of the workings of the economy. Similarly, attempts to abolish differences between social classes through education involves both the adoption of some end, however inadequately formulated, and presupposes some knowledge of the causal connection between education and social class.

The causal view of a community is not, therefore, a rival to the purposive view, since any attempt to achieve social purposes presupposes causal social knowledge. The two views are complementary rather than incompatible and we do not need to say that one is correct rather than the other. It follows that we can ask both how a profession is related causally to the community of which it is a part and how its professional purpose is related to that of the community.

3
THE RELATIONSHIP BETWEEN A PROFESSION AND THE COMMUNITY

i

ON A CAUSAL VIEW OF A COMMUNITY

In the previous section the idea of a community was compared first with that of a person (in (ii)(a)) and then with that of an organism (in (ii)(b)) in order to bring out the sense in which it is that of a totality or complete existent. By contrast, the idea of a profession, like that of an aspect of a person's life such as his membership of a profession, or of an organ of an organism such as the eye of a cat, is that of a part of some larger whole. No account of a profession would be complete, therefore, which did not include an account of the relation between a profession and the community of which it forms a part, just as no account of the eye would be complete which did not include an account of the relation between the eye and the animal body to which it belongs.

The kind of account which is given of the relationship between a profession and the community will depend on whether a causal or a purposive view is taken of a community. The sort of question which arises if a causal view is taken is: 'Does education contribute to national prosperity?'; 'Does the educational system function to maintain a particular class system?'; and so on. Questions of this kind have to be asked if social planning is to be placed on a rational basis, as was pointed out earlier. They are, however, empirical questions, the answers to which lie within the province of sociology rather than philosophy. There might be thought to be philosophical problems about the logical status of the questions themselves; but I hope that what was said earlier provides grounds for claiming that that is not so. It also provides grounds for thinking that no general answer can be given to questions of this kind, even though it can be given to analogous questions in physiology. The causal relations obtaining in each community have to be investigated separately. We cannot assume, for example, that the relation between education and social class obtaining in England obtains also in Japan. What is required to settle these questions, however, is empirical enquiry, not philosophy. For the remainder of this section, therefore, I will consider only the purposive view.

ii

ON A PURPOSIVE VIEW OF A COMMUNITY

I want now, therefore, to consider how a profession is related to the community when a purposive view is taken of a community. It is important to remember, however, that as so conceived a community is an abstraction to which nothing in reality fully corresponds. As pointed out earlier, the causal and purposive views are complementary rather than incompatible, and any actual community will be both causal and purposive.

I have argued that a profession is identified by the purposes which its members share and by the specialised knowledge and skill necessary for their achievement; and that, in view of the logical dependence of means on ends, their identity depends primarily on their purpose. Professions differ from one another, therefore, in the kind of purpose which they pursue and in the knowledge and skills which allow them to do so. Doctors, for example, want their patients to get well; lawyers want justice for their clients; and teachers want their pupils to become educated. Health, justice and education, in other words, are professional values – ways of referring to what different professions want for their respective clients.

A profession, however, exists, and indeed can exist, only as a part of a community. This is a consequence of the kind of thing which it is. For example, since the members of a profession are motivated by an ideal of service to others, there must *be* others to whom they can be of service. Moreover, it was part of the account of a profession that its members not only see themselves as a profession but are also seen as a profession by the rest of the community, their being seen in that way being a necessary condition of their *being* a profession. Again, therefore, there must *be* a community to see them in that way. In recognising them as a profession the community is in effect accepting their offer of service; on the one hand, therefore, the members of a profession think that they have something of value to offer to the community; and, on the other, the community, in recognising them as a profession, is agreeing that this is so. It follows that in the nature of the case professional values are also shared, to a greater or lesser extent, by the rest of the community; in other words, that professional values are also more general social values. This conclusion, although important, is no more than one would expect. Patients want to get well; litigants want justice; and parents want their children to become educated. Nor is there any reason why people who do not expect to benefit directly should not be in favour of health, justice and education. I conclude, then, that a profession is related to the community, both identified by their purposes, through its values, the relation between professional and more general social values being that of partial identity.

iii

PROFESSIONAL VALUES AS SOCIAL VALUES

Social values include the values of every profession in the community as well as others which are not the special concern of any of the professions. This explains why the relation between professional and social values is that of only partial identity.

Professional values, then, form only a part of the total system of values of a community. The question of how a profession is related to the community, therefore, becomes the question of how values are related to each other in a system of social values.

The values which form the parts of a system of social values will

(*a*) be shared values;
(*b*) form a complete system;
(*c*) be intrinsic values;
(*d*) be complementary values;
(*e*) be competitive values.

(a) *Social values as shared values.* In order to form a system of social values, values must be shared by most of the members of a community. In view of the close connection between a system of social values and a community, this condition must be understood in the light of the account of primary social groups in chapter three, section 4(i) and of systems of rules in chapter four section 1. The members of the community must not only share the same values but also be aware that they share them and be aware that they are aware that they share them. This latter phenomenon, whereby the members of a social group form mirrors for each other and, therefore, for themselves, was called reciprocal self-awareness.

(b) *Social values as forming a complete system.* It was argued earlier that the idea of a community is that of a totality with a kind of completeness and self-sufficiency which its parts lack. Similarly, values which form a system in being values of the same community possess the same kind of completeness. A community provides an independently viable way of life for its members; and it is able to do so only because it is based on a set of values which are complete in regulating for every aspect of life in that community. A system of social values, therefore, reflects a view about how life as a whole can and should be lived.

Communities differ from one another in the details of their values. The conditions of human social life, however, are in very general respects fundamentally the same; certain things are bound to be valued, therefore, in any community. Before anything else, men need food and shelter; and as Plato pointed out in the *Republic*, these needs can be met more efficiently through division of labour. Division of labour, however, is pointless without some method of distributing the goods produced by it. Distribution could be effected either bureaucratically or by a system of exchange. Whatever method is adopted, the result must be to confer on individuals the right to consume or enjoy the goods distributed to them; that is, to confer on individuals property in those goods. Moreover, as Hobbes emphasised, men are both vicious and vulnerable and need to be protected from each other. Given the conditions of human existence, therefore, laws safeguarding the enjoyment of property and the security of the person are almost inevitable. One would expect any system of social values, therefore, to include material prosperity and justice.

Education also has a basis in human nature. The membership of a community is constantly changing, owing to the biological processes of birth and death. If the identity of the community is to be maintained, therefore, those born into it must acquire its characteristic ways of looking at things and behaving; and they can do this only by a process of learning from existing members. In small communities in which face-to-face relationships predominate no special provision may be needed to ensure that the necessary learning takes place. In large and complex communities, however, including those which contain recognisable professions, things cannot safely be left to chance and explicit provision must be made for the education of the young.

I have argued that material prosperity and justice are bound to be included in any system of social values; and that a similar, although not quite so conclusive, case can be made for education. Even if these arguments are correct, however, it does not follow that the form which food and shelter take, or the content of laws and the manner of their administering, will be the same. On the contrary, it is obvious that they will not. Each community will have its own traditions of agriculture, manufacture and architecture, and of law and education.

Even if it is possible to produce a minimum list of abstract social values, it is certainly not possible to produce a complete list. Most communities, for example, have some kind of religion; but a wholly secular society is certainly not impossible. A system of values is complete, therefore, only in relation to its parts; just as the life of a person is complete not in any absolute sense but only in relation to its aspects.

(c) *Social values as intrinsic values.* In order to qualify for inclusion in a system of social values, a value must be intrinsic rather than instrumental. I will try to explain the nature of the distinction between intrinsic and instrumental values and go on to say why social values must be intrinsic.

Things may be valued either for their own sake or because they are instrumental in bringing about something else which, in turn, is valued either for its own sake, and may therefore be said to possess intrinsic value, or for the sake of something further. If a regress is to be avoided, therefore, the value of what is of instrumental value must depend on its tendency to lead, sooner or later, to something else which is valued for its own sake.

The world contains many things which people think of as intrinsically valuable, even although they are in no sense the result of human activity; just as it also contains things which are evil but for which man is not responsible. From the point of view of practice, however, the distinction between instrumental and intrinsic values corresponds to that between means and ends of actions. The ideas of means and ends are related in the same kind of way in that nothing counts as a means unless some end to be achieved by it is stated or assumed. A means must be a means *to* something; to think of something as a means, therefore, is necessarily to think of it as contrasted with something else thought of as an end.

It might be said that whoever values the end must also value the means to that end; and, therefore, that it is arbitrary to exclude from a system of social values things which have only instrumental value. The means to be adopted, however, depend not only on the end, but also on contingent factors such as the availability of alternative means to the same end, and the casual relations between means and ends. If these factors were to change or were found to be different to what had been supposed, the view taken of what was of instrumental value would also change even though the same things as before were regarded as of intrinsic value. For this reason, as well as for economy of thought, it is clearly better not to include as social values things which are of only instrumental value.

Values which form part of a system of social values, then, must possess intrinsic value. The overall ends pursued by the different professions all meet this condition. Education, health, justice, security and the arts, for example, are all valued for their own sake, as also is material prosperity.

(d) *Social values as complementary.* In the preceding paragraphs the ideas of instrumental and intrinsic value were contrasted, since to think of something as possessing instrumental value is necessarily to think of it as related to something else thought of as possessing intrinsic value. It might easily be supposed, therefore, that instrumental and intrinsic values are incompatible in that they cannot both be predicated of the same thing without contradiction; in other words, that what possesses instrumental value cannot also possess intrinsic value, and vice versa. This, however, is not so. What is of instrumental value depends, for its instrumental value, on something else thought of as possessing intrinsic value; but this does not exclude its independent possession of intrinsic value. For example, education is undoubtedly of instrumental value in relation to health, justice, security, the arts and material prosperity; but this does not prevent its being regarded as also having intrinsic value. If it is valued in both ways, it is true that the basis of the valuation will be different; but it is nevertheless the same thing which is valued in both ways.

It is possible, therefore, for social values to be both instrumentally and intrinsically valuable. It is also possible for the relation of instrumentality to be reciprocal and, therefore, for two things such as education and material prosperity to be both intrinsically valuable and also of instrumental value in relation to each other. I will call this relation that of complementarity.

The values which form a system of social or community values are characteristically complementary in this sense. For example, only a rich country can afford to spend money on education; and only a country which has a good educational system is likely to become rich. Similarly, commerce is possible only if property is secure; and it is secure only if there is an efficient legal system. Law, therefore, is a source of both justice and prosperity.

It is only fair to point out that social values may be not only complementary but also incompatible. For example, education according to ability and employment according to education are incompatible if adoption of the former policy leads to more highly educated people than there are jobs for them. Similarly, full employment and industrial efficiency are incompatible if full employment causes immobility of labour.

(e) *Social values as competitive.* It is a fact of life that the achievement of human purposes normally requires the use of resources which are scarce in relation to the demands made upon them. For something to be scarce in the relevant sense, it must be limited in supply in the sense that it is not possible to satisfy all the demands which might be made upon it, so that what is used in one way is no longer available to be used in another. And there must be alternative ways in which the same resources might be used. Not everything is scarce in this sense: air, for example, is not, even though it is essential for life. But most things are; for example, building materials and the labour and land needed to make use of them.

It is a consequence of the fact of scarcity that the purposes which a community shares can be realised, in so far as they can be realised at all, only at each other's expense. Social values, therefore, must compete with each other for realisation. Consequently, if the distribution of resources in a community is to be placed on a rational basis, social values must be related to one another by some conception of their relative importance. Since all are regarded as intrinsically valuable, none will be valued to the total exclusion of the rest. But some decision, or rather continuing series of decisions, must be made of their relative importance; for example, of that of education as compared with that of health or security.

4
WHAT VALUES ARE

In the previous section I argued that the relation between a profession and the community of which it is a part could be thought of as either casual or as a relation between purposes; and in connection with the latter view argued that, in the nature of the case, professional values are also more general social values. I went on, therefore, to consider the kinds of ways in which values are related to one another in a system of social values. In line with the argument of chapter four, section 4, what is regarded as valuable in education and the kind of value placed on it will depend on the general social and educational tradition of the society concerned. In our own society, for example, education is valued, *inter alia*, because it produces people who possess knowledge; and knowledge is valued both for its own sake and because it leads to material prosperity.

I want now to try to say something in a general way about the kind of things which values are. There is an almost irresistible temptation to speak of values as though they were part of the furniture of the world, in the sense of existing independently of the people who hold them. And there is, indeed, no objection to saying that values exist, providing the kind of reality which they have is recognised and their dependence for their existence on the people who hold them is not forgotten.

A distinction can be made between personal and shared social values. All values, however, have their foundation in the wants and desires of individuals. Talk about values is a convenient shorthand for talk about the people who hold them and their behaviour. Indeed, I have already pointed out that the distinction between instrumental and intrinsic values corresponds to that between means and ends of actions. In acting, a person is guided not only by beliefs about the situation in which he is acting but also by some conception of the way in which he intends to change it through his action. For a person to hold a value (that is, an intrinsic value) is for him to value some actual or conceivable state of affairs to be maintained or brought about, in so far as it lies within his power to do so. The idea of value, therefore, is that of a relation between a person and the ends of action which he adopts or is disposed to adopt; it is not the idea of an entity which might exist independently of persons. The grammatically appropriate form for a value statement is 'P values X', where 'P' stands for a person and 'X' for a state of affairs; and what it states is that the person concerned is likely to adopt X as one of his purposes. Whether he actually does so will depend both on opportunity and the place of X in his system of values. Some account has already been given of a system of values; to behave in accordance with a system of values is, among other things, to behave in accordance with a stable system of priorities and according to some conception of relative importance.

But although values are founded in this way in the wants and desires of individuals, the distinction between personal values, which might be said to be matters of personal preference and taste, and shared social values, which are not, remains. Values are social phenomena, and in accordance with the argument of chapter three, section 3, therefore, depend for their reality on what they are taken to be. For example, if a person sees value in being able to play the flute, flute-playing has value. But in so far as flute-playing is a matter of personal preference in the society to which he belongs, even if it is a preference which as a matter of fact is held by others, we would not say without qualification that flute-playing has value but that it has value for him. Not all values, however, are like that. Not only are they as a matter of fact shared by all or most of the members of the social group but members of the group are expected and required to share them in being members of that group. For example, we do not say of someone who does not share our concern for personal hygiene that his preferences differ from ours, but that he ought to have a bath. In other words, personal hygiene is not simply valued by some or even most people, but is seen as something which ought to be valued by all members of that social group. And we express this by saying that personal hygiene *is* valuable rather than that it is as a matter of fact valued by most people.

The account of social values sketched out briefly above follows that of social rules in section 1 of chapter four. Rules discriminate among the ways of behaving which would otherwise be open to a person, leaving some to the discretion of the individual but requiring or forbidding others. Similarly, the individual is partly free to value some things and not others according to his own personal preferences; but is required to value others simply in being a member of a particular social tradition or profession. Each individual lives in a social situation which is objectively given so far as he is concerned, even though that situation is created out of the behaviour of the individuals whose situation it is. Individual actions and valuations, therefore, take place against the backcloth provided by a stable social framework. For example, the scientist works in a problem situation which, so far as he is concerned, is objectively given. He does not invent it and cannot ignore it without incurring the penalty of irrelevance and, therefore, being ignored by fellow scientists. His scientific situation is the result of the work of other scientists, past and present. It cannot, however, be reduced to a simple conjunction of their efforts but has a continuing independent existence. The position is similar for other social traditions, including educational. A tradition is built up and maintained by the action and interaction of individuals; but, so far as each individual is concerned, it is something which he did not create and which he must regard as objectively given. He may, indeed, try to modify or change its values but, until he has succeeded in doing so they remain there to be changed.

It might be pointed out, however, that there is a difference in meaning between saying that something *is* in fact valued and saying that it *ought* to be valued or, in other words, that it is valuable. The distinction between what is valued and what is valuable, however, is a third person distinction; it does not hold in the first person, singular or plural. 'I value X' is both factual and evaluative. Anyone who asserts it cannot go on to deny that X is valuable without being guilty of inconsistency. Similarly, 'We, in this community, value X' cannot be followed by 'We, as a social group, do not accept that X is valuable'. In order to deny that what is valued is really valuable a point of view other than that of the individual or group of whom the factual assertion is made must be adopted. It is of course possible to adopt such a point of view; neither 'He values X but X is not valuable' nor 'They value X but X is not valuable' is inconsistent. Both, however, are to be understood as expressing disagreement on the part of the speaker with the value reported to be held by others, rather than as comparing values which are as a matter of fact held by an individual or group with what is objectively valuable irrespective of by whom it is valued, or even of whether it is valued by anyone.

5
CONCLUSION

In this book education has been thought of as a practical social activity and I have tried to explore the form which such a practice would take if its practitioners were members of a profession, that of teaching. It is a consequence of this approach that philosophy of education is thought of as the philosophy of the social practice of education and its primary task as that of understanding that practice.

CHAPTER FIVE: NOTES AND REFERENCES

1(ii) The importance of the point of view of the child is emphasised in the so-called progressive movement in education. See, in this connection, P. S. Wilson's book *Interest and Discipline in Education*.

2. In the *Republic* Plato takes it for granted, in assuming that justice in the individual and justice in the State are the same thing, that the State is like a person. Rousseau also, in introducing the idea of the general will in *The Social Contract*, could be said to be making the same assumption. Aristotle is perhaps the most biologically oriented of philosophers; but, more recently,

it is sociologists rather than philosophers who have taken the comparison between a community and an organism most seriously in adopting the point of view known as functionalism. But what is made of analogies between a State or community and a person or organism obviously depends on the view taken of a person or organism in the first place. Hobbes, for example, thought of the unity of the State as residing in the will of its sovereign and is therefore thinking of the State as like a person. But he also compares a person with a watch and, therefore, is refusing not only to distinguish between a person or animal and a person's or animal's body but also between an animal body and a complex non-organic body.

2(ii)(a) and (iii)(a) The idea of a person as a complete existent and the principle of unity involved in thinking of a person in that way are related to but not the same as the traditional problem of personal identity. A person or self, for example, may be thought of as a bundle of ideas and impressions or a succession of thoughts linked by continuity of consciousness without requiring the ideas of thoughts so linked to constitute a complete existent in the sense indicated in the text.

2(iv) In *The Idea of a Social Science* Professor Peter Winch argues that 'social relations between men exist only in and through their ideas' (p. 123) and that 'social interaction can more profitably be compared to the exchange of ideas in a conversation than to the interaction of forces in a physical system' (p. 128). I am in agreement with these remarks provided they are not linked with the view that because men are socially related in and through their ideas they cannot also be related causally.

4. Professor Peters's view in *Ethics and Education* appears to be that some things possess value independently of their adoption as ends or possible ends by any individual or group of individuals. On his view, therefore, values are to be thought of as properties of things rather than as relations between people and things. I have examined and criticised his view in some detail in 'Values in education', in *New Essays in the Philosophy of Education*, edited by Glenn Langford and D. J. O'Connor.

BIBLIOGRAPHY

Aristotle, *The Ethics of Aristotle – The Nicomachean Ethics*, translated by J. A. K. Thomson, Penguin Classics, Penguin, 1953

Austin, John, *The Province of Jurisprudence Determined* edited by H. L. A. Hart, Weidenfeld & Nicolson, 1954

Bentham, J., *Bentham's Theory of Fictions*, edited by C. K. Ogden, Routledge & Kegan Paul, 1932

— *Introduction to the Principles of Morals and Legislation* in British Moralists, vol. 1, edited by L. S. Selby-Bigge, Dover, 1965

Bradley, F. H., *Ethical Studies*, Oxford University Press, 1876

Descartes, R. *Discourse on Method* and *Meditations on the First Philosophy* Everyman's Library, Dent, 1912

Hare, R. M., *The Language of Morals*, Clarendon Press, 1952

— *Freedom and Reason*, Clarendon Press, 1963

Hart, H. L. A., *The Concept of Law*, Clarendon Press, 1961

Hirst, P. H., and Peters, R. S., *The Logic of Education*, Student Library of Education, Routledge & Kegan Paul, 1970

Hobbes, T., *Leviathan*, edited by M. Oakeshott, Blackwell, 1946

Hoyle, Eric, *The Role of the Teacher*, The Students' Library of Education, Routledge & Kegan Paul, 1969

Hudson, W. D. (ed.), *The Is/Ought Question*, Controversies in Philosophy, Macmillan, 1969

Langford, Glenn, *Philosophy and Education: an Introduction*, Macmillan, 1968

— *Human Action*, Doubleday, 1971

Langford, Glenn and O'Connor, D. J. (eds.) *New Essays in the Philosophy of Education*, International Library of the Philosophy of Education, Routledge & Kegan Paul, 1973

Locke, John, *Enquiry Concerning Human Understanding* edited by A. S. Pringle-Pattison, Clarendon Press, 1924

Melden, A. I., *Free Action*, Studies in Philosophical Psychology, Routledge & Kegan Paul, 1961

Mill, J. S., *Utilitarianism. Liberty Representative Government*, Dent, 1910

O'Connor, D. J., *An Introduction to the Philosophy of Education*, Routledge & Kegan Paul, 1957

Peters, R. S., *Ethics and Education*, George Allen & Unwin, 1966

— (ed.), *The Philosophy of Education*, Oxford Readings in Philosophy, Oxford University Press, 1973

Plato, *The Republic*, edited by F. M. Cornford, Clarendon Press, 1941

Rousseau, J. J., *The Social Contract and Discourses*, translated by G. D. H. Cole, Dent, 1913

Scheffler, I., *The Language of Education*, Charles C. Thomas, 1962

Snook, I. A. (ed.), *Concepts of Indoctrination*, International Library of the Philosophy of Education, Routledge & Kegan Paul, 1972

— *Indoctrination and Education*, Student Library of Education, Routledge & Kegan Paul, 1972

Stevenson, Charles, *Facts and Values*, Yale, 1963

Strawson, P. F., *Individuals*, Methuen, 1959

Tibble, J. W. (ed.), *The Study of Education*, Student Library of Education, Routledge & Kegan Paul, 1966

Urmson, J. O., *Philosophical Analysis*, Clarendon Press, 1956

Wilson, Bryan R. (ed.), *Rationality*, Blackwell, 1970

Wilson, P. S., *Interest and Discipline in Education*, Student Library of Education, Routledge & Kegan Paul, 1971

Winch, Peter, *The Idea of a Social Science*, Studies in Philosophical Psychology, Routledge & Kegan Paul, 1958

Index